BLOODLINES AND BONDS

BLOODLINES AND BONDS

INTERPRETING AND REWORKING PARENT–CHILD DYNAMICS OF ANCIENT GREEK LITERATURE

SHREYOSHI DHAR

B L O O M S B U R Y

NEW DELHI • LONDON • OXFORD • NEW YORK • SYDNEY

BLOOMSBURY INDIA
Bloomsbury Publishing India Pvt. Ltd
Second Floor, LSC Building No. 4, DDA Complex,
Pocket C – 6 & 7, Vasant Kunj,
New Delhi 110070

First published in India 2025

ISBN: 978-93-69526-79-6
2 4 6 8 10 9 7 5 3 1

Printed and bound in India by Replika Press Pvt. Ltd.

to the gods within us,
and the myths we live by …

Contents

Acknowledgements

I owe my success in the completion of my book to my Ph.D. Supervisor, Professor Dr. Soma Banerjee, who has given me the benefit of her precious guidance with her towering knowledge at every step of my work.

I gratefully acknowledge Rabindra Bharati University Library, National Library, Alipore, Kolkata, and Ramkrishna Mission Institute of Culture, Golpark, Kolkata, for providing me ample critical materials for my research work.

I would also like to take this opportunity to convey my deepest gratitude to all my well-wishers, who have helped me a great deal with their honest criticisms, love, and support for my research work. Finally, I would like to extend my sincere gratitude to my friend Dr. Shubham Bhattacharjee for helping out with the paraphernalia associated with the publication of this book.

I

Introduction: Accounting for Variability in Parent–Child Dynamics

... there is nothing either good or bad, but thinking makes it so.
(Shakespeare 99)

There are certain things in the world that are considered to be tabooed but they demand expression. Myths in such cases emerge as being the safety valve for verbalizing such unacceptable abstractions in an acceptable manner. Scholars have disseminated ancient Roman, Greek, Celtic, and Indo-Aryan narratives and literatures to reveal evidences of previously unrecognised psychoanalytic motifs, which find a wide variety of disclosures in later criticisms. The term 'myth' bears a substantial significance in this context. Looking back at the etymology of the term draws our attention to the Greek word μυθολογία (*mythología*), which is a combination of *mȳthos* with the suffix -λογία (*-logia*), meaning 'the telling of stories', 'legends', 'lores' or 'fictions'. The Greek term *mythología* has been borrowed by Fulgentius, a Latin author, in his fifth century book named *Mythologiæ,* where he mentions Greco-Roman etiological narratives involving their deities. The Latin term next finds its place in the Middle French vocabulary as *mythologie* and later the English people adopt the word as *mythology* in the fifteenth century to refer to 'the exposition of a myth or myths'. John Lydgate employs the term for the first time in his book *Troy Boo*k (1425). Thereafter, the term gets its meaning as a moral, fable, parable, anthology of the traditional stories, or allegories. In the early 19th Century, the Greek word Μῦθος (*mȳthos*) has been first used in Anglicised form (myth) as a scholarly term for a traditional story concerned about the genealogy of Gods, kings, and heroes; i.e., the tale of the beginning of the present world or about the primordial beings.

Though myths are generally associated with primitive or pre-scientific people as their cultural tradition, yet interestingly they are often considered as literal truths. Rather than being introduced as engaging fictions, myths are mostly presented as facts. Even for the highly intellectual Greek people, they seem to be actualities. The sceptical part of them have been reconstructed and represented as probable and humane by the authors to make it more acceptable. This seems to have a direct appeal to the man's intuitive faculty as imagination in most cases exerts a strong hold on one's faith and belief. A culture or civilization can never deny its age-old heritage without getting disintegrated. Myths, on being accepted as truths, denote man's awareness of the roots. They comprehend a vivid account of the primitive world; the knowledge and wisdom of the ancient people of a particular place; and the subjects that perplexed and intrigued them. Apart from this, in those narratives, Gods have been presented as personified natural agents like fire, water, Earth, sky, and the like, and therefore, are said to have direct communication with the primitive men. The religious scriptures of the present times recount these narratives which involve how the world has come into being; the various Gods residing there at that time; the powers, the Gods used to have; how those gods have affected the world and the ancient men; and the different methods men used to propitiate those powers. Natural phenomena are moreover explained as the workings of Gods and men have observed certain rites to grant their dreams and desires. Myths often act as the source of various rituals, thereby aiding in adding meaning to it and giving it a supernatural sanction. The Demeter and Persephone myth validates the Eleusinian rites, while Prometheus tricking Zeus gives divine precedence to the fact that men can keep the hide and the meat of a sacrificial animal for themselves, leaving the fat and bones for the Gods. Thus, the ancient myths always have a heavy influence on religion and literature.

Myths have been first reshaped into magnificent literature by literary geniuses like Hesiod, Homer, Aeschylus, Sophocles, Euripides, Aristophanes, Plato, Virgil, Pindar, Horace, Ovid, Apuleius, and others. Classical mythology has been one of the principal constituents for humanistic education throughout the ancient world. Furthermore, from the late Medieval Ages down to the twentieth century, authors from Chaucer to Robert Grave have delved into these narratives for their literary ventures. In case of literature as well as critical theories, rather than viewing mythological motifs in isolation, they can be considered a literary device for presenting characters and plots. The mythological prefiguration in literary texts in such cases thus calls for an awareness of the sources among ideal readers and critics. Similarly, in art, sculpture, and architecture, mythological themes have played quite a significant role. The painters and sculptors of the Renaissance to the Modern age have embraced ideas abound in mythological motifs. Likewise, mythology has been one of the first cultural fields to be traversed by applied psychoanalysis.

The term, 'Psychoanalysis', has been first introduced following the works and theories of an Austrian neurologist Sigmund Freud. Freud is considered to be the father of Psychoanalysis, which is clinically defined as a set of therapeutic techniques dealing with the unconscious mind. All people possess repressed thoughts, feelings, desires, and memories, which give rise to suppressed emotions and these emotions further in their later lives turn into fixations. Psychoanalytic therapy primarily aims to make unconscious conscious as the dynamic unconscious involves those thoughts and feelings which arouse anxiety or self-censure if they become conscious and continues to affect the person's behaviour, attitudes, and experiences in the disguised form of fantasies. It is mostly used as a medical treatment procedure to heal people suffering from depression and anxiety disorder. Sigmund Freud would ask the patients to lie on a couch in a relaxing manner, while he would sit behind listening to their dreams and childhood memories. This would continue for two to five sessions, where he being the analyst would act as a 'blank screen', thereby allowing the clients to utilise the entire space in the relationship to work on their unconscious with no intrusion from outside. In the process, thus he would develop insights into their behavioural patterns, unravelling the meaning of their symptoms, which also includes inkblots, free associations, paraphrases, dream analysis, resistance analysis, and transference analysis.

It is very important to note that psychoanalysis has not only been considered as a medical therapy but also to be a theory, or rather a critical reading method by critics to interpret various literary texts. The theory of psychoanalysis as a criticism assumes that any literary text, very similar to dreams, is the manifestation of the repressed unconscious desires and anxieties of its author. It reflects the creator's own neuroses. The critics' job is to psychoanalyze the characters featured within a literary work, though it is often considered that all the character traits sketched by the authors are projections of their own psyche. The entire approach of this psychoanalytic criticism has been constructed on a literary key for the decoding, and hence, its importance lies in the fact that the particular theory aids in validating the significance of literature. On this note, Freud himself asserted, "The dream-thoughts which we first come across as we proceed with our analysis often strike us by the unusual form in which they are expressed; they are not clothed in the prosaic language usually employed by our thoughts, but are on the contrary represented symbolically by means of similes and metaphors, in images resembling those of poetic speech." (Freud 26)

The approach of Psychoanalytic criticism attempts to disseminate instances of psychological conflicts, ambivalences, guilt, unresolved emotions, and desires, which are important motifs in a literary work. It has been evinced that these psychological traumas are illustrations of the author's own disturbed childhood, family turmoil, sexual conflicts, fixations, which are generally attributed to the characters. These psychological disorders are disguised and encoded indirectly as in case of dreams through 'symbolism', i.e., representation of the repressed objects in disguise; 'condensation', i.e., unification of several thoughts or persons in a single image; and 'displacement', i.e., association of anxiety with other images. Here, in this context, the author and his or her psyche are most important, but psychoanalytic criticism has much similarity with New Criticism from the perspective that both are not concerned with the intention of the author, yet what the author has never intended or the facts that he or she has always tried to suppress, are sought. The unconscious thus has always been attempted to be distorted by the censoring conscious faculty of the mind.

Psychoanalytic criticism has mainly got its prominence since the 1960s among the turmoil, which were witnessed by the post-war period. Freud, upon working with specific sites of the working of human psyche, the instincts, and sexuality, reduces the notion of human individuality into an animalistic sex drive, and thus, together with Karl Marx, Charles Darwin, and Friedrich Nietzsche, destabilized the centres of Western society.

The psychiatrists Jean-Martin Charcot, with his theory of hypnosis, and Joseph Brever's concept of 'taking cure' had exerted considerable influence on the thinking of Sigmund Freud in his proposition of the notion of the unconscious mind, charted in his seminal works like *The Ego and the Id*, *Beyond the Pleasure Principle* (1920), *The Interpretation of Dreams* (1899), *Totem and Taboo* (1913) etc., which has proved to be catastrophic to the Enlightenment ideals or Auguste Comte's 'Positivism' and the other fulcrums of Western rationalism. Psychoanalysis has become one of the most challenging sites of literary criticisms and cultural studies in today's world.

The deep connection between this stream of criticism and the other literary criticisms traversing over much of the twentieth century deals mainly with the articulation of sexuality in language. In this pursuit of the 'literary consciousness', three focal points have been taken into consideration – the author and its corollary character, the reader, and the text. Freud began to focus on the literary text, assuming it to be a symptom of the artist; the association of the author with his or her literary work is analogous to the dreamers' relation to their dreams.

Post-Freudian psychoanalytical Reader Response Criticism is a direct outcome of Freudian theory and analysis, where the psychological experience of the readers in relation to the literary texts is established. This whole concept has been challenged by 'contra-Freud' archetypal criticism of C. G. Jung, which states that a literary work should not be viewed in the context of the writer's or the readers' personal psyche, rather it should be considered as an illustration of how the personal and the collective conscious are related with each other along with the images, symbols, myths, and archetypes of past cultures.

The parent-child paradigm has been an area of considerable interest for psychoanalytic criticism since the recurring theme can traced through myths, legends, tragedies, comedies, and chronicles, involving the Gods, kings, saints, and heroes, down to the modern literature. This particular subject matter has gained enough prominence from the rise of classical studies till present day, yet the deduction or the inference drawn has always been highly prejudiced. The scholars, in order to avoid the consequences, refused to pay heed to the barbarity of the narratives, but later critics have significantly worked upon it. The decade of the 1960s features significant strides towards the target of achieving pertinent variables related to various categories of parent-child relationships. The literature of the time especially served a singular object of elucidating the interconnection or rather the interdependencies of several factors, affecting the value of family relationships.

Literary analysis and criticisms draw their validity from the widely accepted but unexplored premises that states that literary characters are mere reflections of common human beings, exhibiting almost the same behavioural patterns, just like their writers and readers. They share their beliefs, desires, emotions, perceptions, and tendencies. Hence, in lieu of this argument, one can conclude that all literary criticisms can in one or the other way be considered as a psychological criticism and fundamentally a study of human cognition.

Nicholas K. Humphrey asserted that the "novelist is in the most literal sense a 'modeller' of human behaviour, someone whose skill as a psychologist is required not simply to comprehend but to invent the things that other people do." (Humphrey 67) Similarly, drawing on those lines, it can be inferred that a literary critic or a scholar has to be an adept psychologist as this skill helps him or her to perceive the actions of literary characters and narrators of a text along with the operation of their mind. Thus, for the twentieth century critics, Greek society and their narratives have become interesting premises of analysis. The parent-child relationships dealt in those narratives are extensively discussed. They are given psychological explanations and are also interpreted culturally.

Sigmund Freud, at the turn of the century, had published his legendary work *The Interpretation of Dreams* (1899), where he provides a radical new approach to the cure of 'abnormal' adult behaviour, thereby deriving a theory from the narrative of Oedipus recounted in the Greek play, *The Theban Play* by Sophocles, which he terms as 'Oedipus Complex'. Freud explained that a mother is always the primary love-object for a boy, which leads him to desire for a complete union with her, but eventually he abandons this incestuous desire for his mother out of fear of getting castrated by the father and upon realising that females are naturally 'castrated' and hence, he may also suffer the same fate. He accordingly suppresses the incestuous desire, adapts the reality principle, and ultimately longs for being the patriarch, finally identifying with the father and assuming the symbolic role of manhood. Freud had very little to say about girls. He is of the opinion that the girl's route through the Oedipal stage is quite complex. In Freud's view, though the girl begins with getting attached to the mother being caught in a 'homosexual' desire, yet she ends up directing her libido toward her father, upon comprehending the similar castrated state of the mother. When she fails in her attempt, she retires to the mother and tries to identify with her feminine role. Freud was however accused by his contemporaries as well as by his successors for showing very little insight into female sexuality, which he has claimed to be a 'dark continent'. Later, he termed the psychosexuality of girls to be 'Negative Oedipus Complex' or 'Feminine Oedipus Attitude', which has received terrible challenges from critics like Luce Irigaray, Melanie Klein, and others.

The theory of Freud's 'Oedipus Complex' provokes the evolution of Freudian psychology, which seems to have a great impact on several eminent critics like Carl Gustav Jung, Otto Rank, Wilfred Bion, Jacques Lacan and others, who have developed their own ideas and concepts, basing them upon Freud's path-breaking concept. These concepts also have developed into major theories, which have later become important premises for literary criticisms.

Freudian concept of 'Negative Oedipus Complex' or 'Feminine Oedipus Attitude' is later termed by Jung as 'Electra Complex', which leads to a rift between the two gentlemen. Named after the character of Electra, who plotted against her mother to avenge the death of her father, the term refers to the tendency of a girl to possess her father, by competing with her mother. She has to repress these urges and desires from her conscious memory to resolve this dispute in her, and in this process, a number of defence mechanisms are at play.

Both the theories of Oedipus complex and Electra complex, though remained fashionable for a few decades, have lost their mainstream acceptance during 1960s and 1970s. The mainstream academia tends to ignore, or rather reject these ideas. 'Westermarck effect', a modern hypothesis, proposed by Finnish anthropologist Edvard Westermarck in his book *The History of Human Marriage* (1891), offers a reverse sexual imprinting, dismissing children's tendency of incestuous sexual attraction towards their family members or the peers with whom they live with before the age of six, which include their parents as well. It has to be noted that this particular counter theory however fails to secure a place for itself in psychoanalysis. There are still enough subscribers in the field of both the Oedipus complex theory and the Electra complex theory, who blames the rise of the conservative socialist and neo-liberal ideological stances during that time, for the loss of the mainstream acceptance.

The very popular Greek narrative of Demeter and Persephone triggers another important psychoanalytic theory named 'Borderline Personality', though a clinical term, coined by Christine Ann Lawson, is mostly observed in mothers having disturbed childhood, who long to relive it through their relationship with their daughters. This very context has also been utilized by Carl Jung to ascertain the ambivalent relationship between mother and daughter. His theory spells out how a mother has a desire to relive her own maidenhood through her daughter and, at the same time, a daughter also experiences motherhood in the very same relationship. He designates two types of persona for a mother – one being a nurturing mother, who provides life, nourishment, warmth, and security, while the other being a terrible mother, who at the anticipation of getting separated from her child, acts as a hindrance to their marriage. Apart from Demeter, the narrative of Aphrodite also obliges her to fit into the category of a terrible mother. A marriage not only impacts the life of the child but also the mother has to suffer as a result of being distanced from her child. The boy, from his very adolescence, starts to experience a feeling of separateness from his mother naturally due to his masculinity, but a daughter seems to stay undistinguished in a mother-daughter enmeshment for a much longer time period, according to Helen Luke in her article "The Mother-Daughter Mysteries".

The parent-child relationships in Homer's works are quite unique. A strong emotional bonding can be witnessed. Children, especially the sons, have lot of respect for their fathers, and at the same time, the fathers are also proud of their sons. Sons even sacrifice their lives to save their father's reputations and follow their footsteps of being noble warriors. The sons in *Iliad* are mostly defined by their fathers' names and ancestral loyalty is one of the main themes explored in the text. Both the *Iliad* and the *Odyssey*, apart from being a major story about war, also depicts exclusively strong paternal and maternal relationships among fathers and sons and mothers and sons respectively, along with ancestral loyalty among characters. Thus, these heroic epics offer a new outlook to the Homeric society. The term 'threptra' is a cultural and ethical construct, in which sons repay their parents for rearing them by taking care of them in their old age. In *Odyssey*, Telemachus is found to put his own life at risk for bringing back Odyssey, while Achilles pays his threptra to Priam, considering him to be a substitute for his own father. Unfortunately, Hippothus, Sinoeisius, and Hector could not pay their threptra for their untimely death. Again in *Oedipus at Colonus*, the daughters are found to play the role of the sons as they are busy fighting for kingship. This concept of threptra was validated both by law and society in the age of Homer.

Mythology has always been the epicentre of every civilization; people of all generations have to rely on the prevalent myths for their knowledge about religion, history, and morality. Literature itself has evolved from mythology. Authors of all places and languages have more often than not employed allegories, metaphors, and analogies in their works, borrowing the motifs and themes from the myths of a particular culture or location. Greek and Roman myths have never been published in English, though several translations have been done later, yet they have considerable influence over not only the English literature, but also over the entire Western literature as a whole. Numerous mainstream authors of English literature have referred to Greek and Roman mythology to enhance the eminence of their works. The authors of all ages, starting from Shakespeare to the modern-day writers, have been fascinated by the myths of their Greek Roman predecessors. Under the guise of presenting the myths, they often recounts narratives featuring concealment, treachery, or hidden motives, and escape from being tabooed.

This book intends to explore the ancient Greek and Roman narratives, where the theme of parent-child relationship occupies a central position. These narratives are further reconstructed into literatures of various genres and a vivid psychoanalytic and cultural reading of them have been attempted mainly by the eminent twentieth century critics and theorists, thereby developing various psychological theories, later used as motifs in various texts. The selection of parent-child relationship as a subject of investigation has been done since it has always been a fundamental phenomenon in human life and subsequently in Literature.

Works Cited

Freud, Sigmund. "On Dreams." *Art in theory, 1900-1990: An Anthology of Changing Ideas.* Edited by Charles Harrison and Paul Wood, Blackwell Publishers Ltd, 1992.

Humphrey, Nicholas K. *Consciousness Regained.* Oxford UP, 1983.

Shakespeare, William. *The Tragedy of Hamlet, Prince of Denmark.* Simon & Schuster, 1992. https://shakespeare.folger.edu/. Accessed 16 May. 2022.

II

Parallel Patterns in Two Pairs of Complexes: Oedipal and Electra Behaviours/Schemas

The Judaeo-Christian interval seems to have been both occupied and illuminated by the Greek civilization and so the discipline of psychoanalysis has felt more inclined toward the Greek civilization than to any other. There is probably no other period in history at which scholars have thrown more light on as the Greeks due to their detailed projection of divinities; the concrete controversy of desire, which leads to several instances of struggles for the possession of a woman resulting in several murders and violence; betrayals of vows and pledges; the grieves and wounds of unfulfilled love; ruthless tortures against adversaries; squabble between the imperishability of alliances in common sacrifice and thereby getting resentful of one another for sharing the magnificent conquests; the quest for power and position and the greed for its acknowledgment by putting on its insignia; the challenge to the establishment of divine and human laws; demonstration of outstanding courage at the point of death; the conflict between duty and emotion, nation and family, and law and heart; and the overreaching drive that compels the heroes to progress towards attainment of truth or for the illumination of some that have either devastated or receded. In all these rapid proliferation and outgrowth of myths, tragedy seems to be the most appropriate method of decanting them, helping them to settle, and in turn attempts to fix them in one particular artistic form. Though, it does not always confront the subject directly, yet it aids into both expressing as well as in concealing the raw matter from the readers and audiences. Thus, the cycles of Argos and Thebes have proved to be important models to refer to. The creative works of Aeschylus, Sophocles, and Euripides similarly cannot evade the méconnaissance or misinterpretation that marks every motif with respect to the signifiers they have delivered.

In complete contrast to the present archetypes of parent-child relationships, the Greek and the Roman myths have evinced that incest at one point of time gained social acceptance. We can find several instances of twisted relationships in those narratives – mothers and sons are found to be sharing exceptionally strong bonds; parents are often threatened and even sometimes executed by their children and vice-versa; and betrayal of one another has been the most frequently dealt theme. Many such activities and ideas considered to be tabooed by today's society were given validation during the classical age, among which, parents and children sharing unusual, distorted, and dysfunctional relationship is counted to be one. Generally, it is an accepted notion that parents should care and sacrifice for their young ones, but in Greek and Roman mythology, killing one's children or filicide was not believed to be forbidden, especially if there is a grave motive behind it or if it is by any means necessary to secure a higher status. Both the Romans and Greeks considered it very important to keep a high social reputation as they always had high esteem for the ones having great power. Mostly instances are found where mothers get into real conflict with the fathers, who strive to retain control and refuse to pass it over even to their own progeny. This circumstance often leads to tension among the members of the family. In this manner, we can witness that the family relationships of the Gods and of the mortals are quite alike in ancient Greek and Roman society, thereby compelling these unruly behaviours to appear more acceptable.

Being born in ancient Greek and Rome, the citizens have been raised hearing the myths, which cause them to understand and believe that they are not very much different from the Gods and hence, they should act and behave accordingly and must have the same personalities and habits. There was a saying in ancient Greek philosophy that Homer has created Gods, who acted quite selfishly and were motivated by emotions like favouritism and jealousy, just like average human beings. They were much similar to ordinary people, barring the fact that they were immortals, having supernatural powers. They made human errors and were prone to commit heinous crimes and this distinguished them from the Gods of other religions. Following them, the ancient Greeks and Romans found it a lot easier to be humane and commit mistakes, rather than to try to achieve perfection and be sinless.

As with the case of Homer, Hesiod, an ancient Greek epic poet of Boeotia, seemed to be quite eminent in the 8th century B.C., though unlike Homer, some of his biographical details are likely to have been gathered from the poet's own canonical works like *Theogony*, *Works and Days*, and others. His father hailed from Kyme in Aeolis, a region located between Ionia and Troad in north-western Anatolia, but they settled at Boeotian Asara, which he described as "a cursed place, cruel in winter, hard in summer, never pleasant" in *Works and Days*. (Hesiod 640) He also mentioned about a small piece of land at the foot of Mount Helicon, his patrimony, which created a legal dispute with his brother Perses, who won both the lawsuits under the same judges. This mountain had always been a source of poetic inspiration as according to him the Muses reside there.

Hesiod's first major composition *Works and Days* revolves around two major ideas – one being that labour is the universal lot of Man, while the other being, one who is willing to labour will get by. This long poem is set against the background of agrarian crisis in the mainland of Greece, which provoked a series of documented colonization in search of a new land. His second major work *Theogony* though composed earlier is considered to be one of the most vital sources of understanding of the ancient Greek culture and civilisation. It concerns the beginning of the world as well as the origin of the Gods, worshipped in those days. The series of narratives involving the genealogy of Gods later develops into a wave of myth, which inspired a host of later literary works and critical theories. Scholars generally believe that Hesiod may have drawn his inspiration for his texts from other eastern succession myths like Akkadian-Babylonian creation epic, the "Enuma Elish" and the Hurrian-Hittite "Kingship in Heaven". Both the epic poems of Hesiod illuminate the readers about the nature of Greek mythology in totality. Interestingly, Hesiod makes an important assertion in his works that he as a poet has been bestowed the sole authority and responsibility of dispersing the narratives of cosmology and theogony by the Muses directly, thereby proclaiming himself as a prophet for the upcoming generation.

Throughout the first major work of Hesiod, *Theogony*, the poet-narrator recounts an extensive detailed chronology of different Gods and Goddesses, categorising them and their genealogies, and elucidating their relations to one another. Parent-child paradigm has been one of the fundamental motifs explained in the text.

The poem, like any other epic poetry, begins with invoking the Muses, claiming that they themselves have descended once to visit him and to teach him 'fine singing'. Here, he informs about the origins of these Muses and explains how they benefit men, who are their favourites, by giving them good judgement, lucid speech, and reverence from peers. Next, he moves on to describe how Chasm and Earth spontaneously come into existence out of nothingness, i.e., the Chaos, and then Tartara or Tartarus (the Underworld), Gaia (the Earth), Eros (the Sexual Desire), Erebus (Darkness), and Nyx (Night) follow them. Erebos and Nyx give birth to

Aither (Brightness) and Hemera (Day), while from Gaia and Ouranos, or Uranus (Sky), Ourea (Mountains), and Pontus (Sea) come into being. Three categories of offspring are born from the union of Ouranos and Gaia – the twelve Titans and Tethys, who have ruled the Golden Age; a race of one-eyed giants called Cyclops; and three Hecatoncheires (Cottus, Briareus and Gyges) having a hundred arms each. Witnessing the ferocity and fearsome appearance of the children, Ouranos feels compelled to lock them with their mother Earth in a cave, weary of the threat that they might pose against his kingship. He only visits the cave to satisfy his sexual cravings. This disgusts Gaia so much that she has sought help from the Titans in punishing her husband, but no one have paid heed to her request, except the youngest and most ambitious Kronos or Cronus. Gaia crafts an adamantine sickle and gives it to Kronos, who ambushes Ouranos and castrates him with it, thereby assuming the throne in his stead. Ouranos's blood splashes on Gaia and from the drops, Erinyes (the vengeful Furies), the Gigantes (Giants), and the Meliai (three nymphs) are born. Kronos disposed Ouranos's disrupted testicles into the sea, and from there, Aphrodite (the Goddess of Love) originates.

Hesiod continues with the narrative, citing the genealogy of Gods, who have given birth to numerous Gods, Goddesses, nymphs, heroes as well as monsters. Then, a vivid account of the children born to Kronos and Rhea contributes to the progression of the narration of succession. The guilt of the execution of his father continues to torment Kronos, who fears of sharing the same fate and therefore he hatches a plan to escape it. He begins swallowing each of the children born to his mate Rhea. Helplessly, Rhea has to find out a way to save her progeny. When she bears Zeus, she gives him to Gaia to raise him, tricking Kronos into swallowing a stone being wrapped with a child's cloth. Meanwhile, Zeus grows up on the unknown island of Crete. When he returns as an adult, he too tricks his father to spit back all his siblings that he has engulfed soon after they have been born.

The tale thereafter recounts the war between Zeus and the other Olympians on one side and Kronos and the Titans on the other side. Other Gods and Goddesses including Obriareos, Kottos, and Gyges have helped Zeus in overthrowing his rivals. Zeus locks the Titans in Tatarus finally to avoid any further conflict. This is followed by a detailed description of the descendants of the Olympians. Earth also gives birth with Tartarus to a new opponent of Zeus, Typhoeus. Zeus again wages a war against Typhoeus and easily obliterates him.

History starts to repeat again as Zeus feels threatened by his own children. When Athena, his first child, is about to take her birth through his first wife Metis, he swallows her and gives her birth out of his head instead. At the end of the epic poem, stories about the genealogies of various other mythological characters are narrated, who have given birth to prominent mythological figures having both divine and human progenitors.

Hesiod's other notable work *Works and Days*, very similar to *Theogony*, is crowned with chronicles featuring several parent-child narratives. The literary piece serves as a didactic poem and dates back to approximately the 8th century BCE. It starts as usual by invoking the Muses, pleading them to bestow through their melodious song and to dedicate a hymn to their father Zeus, who is in charge of all consequences. Hesiod, being the poet-narrator, also requests his brother Perses to hear all about truth and justice that he will be recounting in his narrative. Next, he states that in the world there are two categories of conflicts or competitions – one that is commendable and the other being reprehensible. While the reprehensible strife "promotes ugly fighting and conflict" (Hesiod 37), the commendable ones are designed by Zeus for man's benefit, which encourages success and instigates the competitive nature in them. Here, he implores Perses to "lay this down in your heart" so that "strife who exults in misfortune" (Hesiod 37) does not deviate his focus from his mission by instigating him to get involved in any kind of disputation. He also accuses his brother of bribing the elders to help him have a larger share of their family estate, which is unfair on him and hence Perses must "settle [the] dispute with straight judgements" (Hesiod 38) from Zeus.

Hesiod next narrates the legend of Prometheus to preach the reason why work should be just and why it is important. Gods earlier are known to have a tendency to conceal man's food as a punishment of taking the help of Prometheus. Zeus gets to know about this treachery of Prometheus and as a further punishment, he hides fire from men, which again has been stolen by Prometheus against the wish of Zeus. In rage, he makes a plan to present something that will appear as a delight but upon accepting, it will cause them to "embrace their own misfortune" (Hesiod 38). According to his instruction, Hephaestus curves out a beautiful woman, mixing earth and water to which Athena teaches her crafts; Aphrodite imparts in her the art of arousing "painful yearning and consuming obsessions" (Hesiod 38); and Hermes gives her "a knavish nature" (Hesiod 38) and names her Pandora. Zeus then orders Hermes to gift Pandora to Epimetheus, Prometheus's brother. Prometheus, suspecting a conspiracy, warns his brother not to accept anything from the Gods, "lest some application befall mortals" (Hesiod 39), but Epimetheus, unable to control his lust, accepts Pandora. Soon, Pandora unstops the jar, containing 'suffering', 'toil', and 'sickness', which were till then unknown to men, thereby unleashing these ills upon them. Later, Zeus himself helps her to recover the jar before it gets lost. This further establishes the fact that creators have often got engaged in a battle with their own creation, and vice-versa; the parent-child paradigm is not always peaceful.

The Prometheus myth is followed by another tale, which narrates how Gods and mortals have sprouted from the same starting point. The first race of men is created by the Titans, especially Kronos, whom the Romans called by the name of Saturn. This time period has been termed the 'Golden Age'. Men at that time had been completely unaware of sorrow or labour; their death had been like falling asleep. They never had to toil or grow unhappy or dissatisfied. The season of spring had never ceased to exist in the age. People had seemed to age backward and they had died as 'daimones' (the Greek word translated later as 'demons'), who wandered on the earth. The age came to an end with the overcoming of the Titans by Zeus.

This age was followed by the 'Silver Age', which was in charge of the Olympian Gods. The created mortals appeared to be much inferior in both appearance and wisdom. There were four seasons in a year. Adult men had to work in the field for their appetite and seek their shelter but a child had hundred years to enjoy before growing up. This race could never honour or satisfy the Gods and so Zeus destroyed them himself. After their death, they became sacred spirits of the underworld.

Next follows the 'Bronze Age', when man had been created from ash trees, which had been used to make spears. The people of this age were of violent and ruthless nature. They had made their weapons and houses from bronze and had always consumed meat instead of bread. They had been destroyed by flood in the times of Prometheus's sons, Deucalion and Pyrrah. Like the early men, they too had been fated to go underground after their death. Since, mortals of these three ages had their final destination in the underworld; the metals, gold, silver, and bronze are to be found underground.

The fourth age is the heroic age, also called the 'Age of Heroes'. Men in that age had been called Hemitheoi and had been like demigods, being strong, brave, and heroic, but most of them had been destroyed during the great wars of the Greeks. After their death, some get their place in the underworld, while the others in the islands of the blessed ones.

Hesiod names his own time as the 'Iron Age'. Zeus has created all men of the fifth age with evil and selfish traits and has burdened them with weariness and sorrows. All forms of evils have come into existence in this time period. All the virtues seem to disappear and so, all the Gods, who remained on Earth, have left it. Hesiod wishes that Zeus will surely put an end to this race someday. He laments for belonging to this tribe, though he himself affirms that it has "good mixed with ill". (Hesiod 42) According to him, when babies will be born with grey hair, Zeus will destroy them and they will subside into discord, violence, lawlessness, injustice, and indecency.

After this vivid description of the ages, Hesiod offers other advices, which are specially directed towards his brothers; this includes avoiding dishonest means to deceive the weaker ones, being kind with friends, earning through labour instead of bribing to acquire gifts, practicing restraints, offering and sacrificing to please the Gods and Goddesses, honouring them, and thus directs all to lead a pious life. He uses several fables to establish his arguments. Many superstitious practices and customs are also mentioned and dealt in details. The plot of the didactic poem *Works and Days* is thus in accord with the previous work *Theogony*'s deviation from an anarchic polytheism.

Hesiod, in his major works, thus portrayed that the relationship between Gods and their sons is quite peculiar. They are violent with each other and in this manner, they failed to provide the archetype for a healthy bond between fathers and sons. This cosmic turbulence in the succession myths reveals two vital moments of tension between a father and a son, i.e., at the time of the child's birth and at the prime of the son's youth, which provide a fitting model for the works of the later Greek playwrights like Aeschylus, Sophocles, Euripides and others. Apart from Hesiod, Homer, Cinaethon, and other known figures of the oral tradition of literature also contributed their versions of the motif, which served as a prototype for the chronicles of those Greek authors. The most famous legend is the Oedipus myth, which has numerous versions of classical artistic depictions like plays, poems, etc.

The Oedipus story first finds its mention in the works of Homer. The epic poems *Odyssey* and *Iliad* give a reference of the tale of Oedipus, though much detail has not been given anywhere. Both the two timeless extant works of literature, widely read by modern audience, the *Odyssey* and the *Iliad*, are set against the background of the Trojan War, which have resulted due to a clash among the Mycenaean Greek kingdoms. The main focus of the *Iliad* is the brawl which sparked between the two great warriors Agamemnon and Achilles during the last year of the war, while the *Odyssey* recounts the story of the king of Ithaca Odysseus's return journey back home after the Trojan War. Both the ancient epic poems are counted among the earliest surviving literatures, which serve as sources of many mythical narratives, upon which latter plays, poems, stories, and other forms of literature are based.

There is a funeral game, designed to honour the death of Patroclus, about which is recounted in an episode near the end of *Iliad*. The name of Oedipus for the first time is uttered as a passing name, checked during the funeral, when the particular episode is further related in *Odyssey*, Book XI. Odyssey amuses his Phaiakian hosts by narrating a conversation with Epikaste or Epicaste, whom he has met in the underworld along with many other departed souls. The spirit of Epicaste, while unfolding her crisis, tells him that unknowingly she has married her son Oedipus soon after he kills his father. The whole truth gets unravelled whereupon Epicaste hangs herself out of guilt and shame, while Oedipus continues to rule over Thebes. After having the conversation, he attempts to meet with his fallen comrades of Troy just when he comes face-to-face with a parade of women, whose names he begins to catalogue for his audience, which includes Oedipus's mother Epicaste.

> And I saw the mother of Oedipus, beautiful Epicaste.
> What a monstrous thing she did, in all innocence—
> she married her own son …
> who'd killed his father, then he married her!
> But the gods soon made it known to all mankind.
> So he in growing pain ruled on in beloved Thebes,
> lording Cadmus' people—thanks to the gods' brutal plan—
> while she went down to Death who guards the massive gates.
> Lashing a noose to a steep rafter, there she hanged aloft,
> strangling in all her anguish, leaving her son to bear
> the world of horror a mother's Furies bring to life. (Odyssey 183)

This little piece of material practically frustrated the scholars of the period due to lack of sufficient information, and hence they turned their attention to other later sources to reconstruct the myth in totality. In the narration of Homer, there is no mention of either the oracle or the Sphinx. There has been a hint only about Oedipus killing his father and thereafter getting married to his mother. He later dies in exile.

> The giant spoke; and in a stupid gaze
> The host beheld him, silent with amaze!

> 'Twas thou, Euryalus! who durst aspire
> To meet his might, and emulate thy sire,
> The great Mecistheus; who in days of yore
> In Theban games the noblest trophy bore,
> (The games ordain'd dead Oedipus to grace,)
> And singly vanquish the Cadmean race. (Homer 695)

Hesiod was the first poet to mention about Sphinx, though there was no mention of Oedipus there.

> Echidna was subject in love to Orthus and brought forth the deadly Sphinx which destroyed the Cadmeans and the Nemean lion, which Hera, the good wife of Zeus, brought up and made to haunt the hills of Nemea, a plague to men. (Hesiod 330)

A Sphinx is a female monster having the body of a lion and the head and the breast of a woman. In Greek mythology, she is often known to be a daughter of Orthus and Chimaera or Echidna, born in the nation of the Armi. Hesiod also mentions about a three-legged old man, who later becomes the part of the Sphinx riddle. Another ancient poet of Sparta named Cinaethon wrote another epic poem *The Story of Oedipus*, commonly called *Oedipodea*, which is found only in portions as the complete text did not survive. The few scattered fragments retrieved give evidence of the fact that Cinaethon was the first author to combine the story of Oedipus with the Sphinx's riddle into one single narrative, but the detailed account of the chronicle could not be recovered. An anonymous work has also been discovered titled *The Thebaid*, which first tells about the curse that befall upon the sons of Oedipus and how they end up killing each other.

> Then the hell-born hero, golden-haired Polyneices, first played beside Oedipus a rich table of silver which once belonged to Cadmus the divinely wise: next he filled a fine golden cup with sweet wine. But when Oedipus perceived these treasures of his father, great misery fell on his heart, and he straight-way called down bitter curses there in the presence of both his sons. And the avenging Fury of the gods failed not to hear him as he prayed that they might never divide their father's goods in loving brotherhood, but that war and fighting might be ever the portion of them both. (*The Thebaid*)

> And when Oedipus noticed the haunch he threw it on the ground and said: "Oh! Oh! my sons have sent this mocking me ..." So he prayed to Zeus the king and the other deathless gods that each might fall by his brother's hand and go down into the house of Hades. (*The Thebaid*)

Even this text does not exist in its entirety. The Roman poet Publius Papinius Statius wrote a parallel story featuring the same title, which is preserved still.

In the 5th century BCE, many Greek playwrights attempted to use the Oedipus story in their own literary art forms. Unlike the earlier fragmented versions, these plays chronicle Oedipus's rise to power in vivid details, though they often vary from each other on various points. More or less a plot had been developed, describing the events that lead to the tragic fate of Oedipus. Laius, the king of Thebes, has been prophesied to be killed in the hands of his own son. Getting terrified, he pierces Oedipus's feet after he is born and sends him into a place outside Thebes, leaving him there to die, but fortunately the boy is rescued by a herdsman, who takes him out of Thebes. When he grows up, again due to a prophecy, that he will be killing his father and marrying his mother, he has set out to solve the riddle given by a Sphinx. On his venture, he comes across Laius and a fight breaks off in which he kills Laius. He then becomes the king after defeating the Sphinx and unknowingly marries his mother. This calls upon a plague on the Thebans. When the truth gets discovered, Oedipus blinds himself and Jocasta commits suicide by hanging herself. The narrative ends with the sons of Oedipus, killing each other.

The new versions of the narrative differ from the older versions of the myth as the ending of the new versions recount the stepping down of Oedipus from the throne, while the older versions of the myth end with Oedipus being killed in the battle. Apart from that, initially it has been said that Oedipus has children by his second wife, but in the later versions, all his children are attributed to Jocasta. Earlier, Jocasta has been known by the name of Epicaste, which is no longer used since 5th century BCE.

The next known adaptation of the Oedipus myth after Homer is the second Olympian Ode by Pindar.

> Laios' tragic son, crossing his father's path, killed him and fulfilled the oracle spoken of old at Pytho. And sharp-eyed Erinys saw and slew his warlike children at each other's hands. Yet Thersandros survived fallen Polyneikes and won honor in youthful contests and the brunt of war, a scion of aid to the house of Adrastos. (Pindar)

In the 5th century BCE, Greek theatre was completely different from the modern concept of theatre. While performances in the modern theatre are mainly for entertainment purpose, the theatre in the Greek society was part of a religious festival. Dionysus, an ancient deity, residing in the wild, was famous for his subversive revelry. He was attributed to both drunkenness as well as sexuality and was the one mainly worshipped through the theatrical performances of the time. Citizen of the then society participated or attended those theatres as an act of worship. The spring season was considered to be the season of Dionysus and the plays were mostly enacted at the beginning of this season. At the end of the annual festival, judges would assess the performances.

The Athenian playwright Aeschylus in 467 BCE introduced a trilogy *Seven Against Thebes* on the Oedipus legend, which won the first prize at the city of Dionysia. The first play was named *Laius*, the second *Oedipus*, while the third *Seven Against Thebes*. The last play was the only one to have survived and it recounts how the third generation, i.e., the sons of Oedipus, Eteocles and Polynices, war against each other for the throne and end up killing one another. The trilogy gives a detailed account of the miseries suffered by the three successive generations of the royal family of Thebes. It is followed by a satire play titled *The Sphinx*.

In 429 BCE, Sophocles, considered being the greatest playwright in Athens, presented his first play onstage *Oedipus the King*, followed by the second *Oedipus at Colonus*, which was supposed to be the third written play of the trilogy *The Theban Play*, and last came the first of the series *Antigone*. He has given special efforts in compressing the elements of the story into the Aristotelian unities, thereby exploring the tragic fate of Oedipus.

The play *Oedipus the King* begins with the Theban people seeking help from the king as they are terribly suffering due to a plague, from which they can be rescued only if the cause of the plague has been discovered. Creon after visiting the Oracle has just returned to Thebes while Apollo reveals that the plague will be lifted on one condition, i.e., if the old king Laius's murderer is found and executed. Oedipus decides to fulfil it at any cost. Tiresias, the blind foreteller, after much persuasion, lays the bare truth that it is Oedipus himself, who is the main culprit, but Oedipus continues to deny it and views it as a cunning design made by Creon to usurp the throne. In the second scene, Oedipus begins to doubt as Jocasta mentions that Laius has been slain at the crossroad on that very same day in which Oedipus stepped into Thebes for the first time. Upon hearing that there is one survivor who has been the eyewitness of the event, he immediately sends for the man, hoping that he may deny his guilt. Scene III begins with the news of King Polybus, Oedipus's foster father's death, which brings him some momentary relief as he has always known Polybus to be his biological father, who he is destined to kill.

Unfortunately, the messenger who has brought the news, affirms that he is the man who has given baby Oedipus to the childless king many years ago when he finds him alone in the pass of Kithairon, and the servant, for whom Oedipus is waiting to identify Laius's murderer, is the very same man, who under the king's order has taken Oedipus up to the mountain, where the messenger has found him. Jocasta immediately tries to stop pursuing the matter further as she can relate to the incident clearly, but Oedipus remains firm and refuses to pay any heed to her request. The truth gets uncovered at once. This seems too much for Oedipus to bear his cruel fate and hence he rushes into the palace only to find his mother and wife hung by her own hands. Extremely ashamed of the whole situation, Oedipus rips a brooch from her dress and blinds himself with it. He next pleads Creon to exile him from the kingdom. He also asks him to give permission to take his two daughters Antigone and Ismene with him but he instantly denies this; instead, he orders him to wander alone for the rest of his life.

Oedipus at Colonus is the second play of the series to be performed though it is written at last just before Sophocles' death and it is the largest play of the trilogy. The play depicts how the tragic hero Oedipus' life comes to an end and how he bears mythic significance for Athens in his last days, capable of bestowing divine blessings through his extra-celestial power.

Banished from his own kingdom Thebes, Oedipus emerges to be a beggar at the start of the play. Antigone accompanies him to Colonus, a city very close to Athens, where they have reached a ground considered sacred to the furies or Eumenides. He wishes to meet the king of Athens Theseus, while Ismene, his younger daughter, brings news that Creon and Eteocles, Oedipus' son, have requested Oedipus to spend his last days in Thebes so that they can escape the forthcoming cruel fate as anticipated by the oracle. Oedipus immediately declines the request, asserting that he has earlier promised Theseus to have the divine grace if he allows him to die and be buried in the city of Colonus and Theseus has willingly granted all his wishes. When Creon makes his daughter hostage and threatens to wage a war for Oedipus' return, Theseus gives Oedipus full protection, rescues his daughters, and drives Creon out of the city. Polynices, Oedipus's other son, arrives soon after Creon is sent out. He pleads his father's support in regaining the crown from Creon and Eteocles. Notwithstanding this anarchic situation, Oedipus curses that both the brothers will be killed at each other's hands. All of a sudden, a sound of thunder is heard and Oedipus can sense that his death is near. He takes his two daughters and Theseus to a secret part of the grove and gets ready for death to come. Theseus was the only person to witness the ending of Oedipus's life. As prophesied, Athens gains the divine blessing and grace while Thebes suffers his curse. The play ends with both Antigone and Ismene returning to Thebes in order to prevent the civil war.

The third play to be enacted onstage was the *Antigone*, though it is the first one to be written by Sophocles. The play opens with the violent strife in Thebes in which Eteocles and Polynices kill each other as cursed by their father Oedipus and the city remains unconquered. The audiences also get to know from the conversation of Antigone and Ismene that Creon is preparing to give Eteocles a proper burial as he dies defending the crown of the city, while Polynices shall be considered as an invader and hence his body must be left to rot. Creon has also issued a stern warning that who attempts to do the last rites of Polynices will be stoned to death in public. Antigone reveals to Ismene that she has decided to offer a ritual burial to Polynices secretly, but when Ismene refuses to disobey the king's order, she plans to do the needful alone without the help of anyone.

Soon, it has been discovered that an attempt has been made to bury Polynices by Antigone. Creon immediately orders to put her into trial but Antigone argues that it is Creon himself who has denied the laws of Gods and thus refuses to surrender her own self to his authority. The enraged Creon instantly declares that she and her sister will receive a death sentence. Meanwhile, Haeman, the son of Creon and betrothed of Antigone, requests his father to reconsider his decision. Hearing this, Creon blames his son of having an unmanly weak personality. This angers Haeman and he leaves with a promise that he will never return. Thereafter, Creon rephrases his verdict, pronouncing that Ismene shall be forgiven but Antigone will be locked in a tomb and left to die in starvation instead of being stoned to death. Tiresias, getting to know about Antigone's execution, warns Creon that if Polynices' body does not receive a proper funeral and burial, the Gods may punish him with the same curse and that he also has to suffer his own son's death. Unwillingly, Creon decides to bury Polynices and pardon Antigone, but it gets too late. A series of death follows thereafter. Antigone hangs herself, and upon hearing this, Haeman kills himself in grief, which is followed by Eurydice, the queen's suicide. Creon holds himself responsible for the tragic fate of the whole family and craves for a quick death. At the end of the play, the chorus sings a sombre warning that pride can never escape the blow of destiny.

The legend of Oedipus has also been retold into the plays of Euripides titled *Phoenissae* and *Chrysippus*. In *Phoenissae*, Jocasta begins the narrative, recalling the tale of Oedipus. An attempt has been made by Euripides to merge the plots of the plays *Seven Against Thebes* and *Antigone* into one single play. He has changed the plot in two aspects – the first, the reason behind the brawl between Laius and Oedipus has not been recorded earlier in any version, but it is described here in details. Laius orders Oedipus to move from his path, while his chariot passes through the crossroad. Proud and arrogant Oedipus considers it to be demeaning on his part to give way to any other man and hence, he refuses to comply. This results in a feud between the two in which Oedipus slays Laius. The second point where Euripides has brought about some alteration is that even after learning about the truth that Oedipus actually is her son and her husband's murderer, Jocasta does not kill herself and Oedipus has also not fled into exile; rather they both attempt to try to delay their fate. It is the fatal strife of Eteocles and Polynices that compels Jocasta to hang herself and Oedipus leaves for exile with Antigone.

Chrysippus provides a detailed account of the backdrop of the curse that befell on Laius. He commits a tricked crime in the past of absconding Chrysippus, the son of Philip, in order to disregard him, and for this the Gods have cursed his whole family to be doomed.

Euripides is known to have written another play on the same subject *Oedipus*, but only fragments of it have been recovered. The first line of the prologue pronounces that Laius has been damned since he conceives a son against the wish of Apollo. Another striking variation to be noticed in this version is that Oedipus has been blinded by Laius's attendants long before he has been identified as Laius's son.

The adventure of Oedipus has been probably the most frequently used motif for classical literature. Several versions of the chronicle can be traced, though many survive only in fragments. Even Julius Caesar has been known to have written a play on Oedipus, but it has not been preserved. The figure of Oedipus has been given much attention timelessly since the theme of father-son rivalry reached its zenith in this narrative, even though Homer and Hesiod have portrayed the issue quite vividly in their masterpieces.

The second-century dream analyser Artemidorus of Daldi is probably the first one to ponder upon incestuous dreams. According to him, the dreamer's social predicament should be taken into consideration while interpreting his unnatural dreams. The twentieth-century psychoanalyst Sigmund Freud shared a similar interest in such matters but significantly differed in his interpretation. He believed that human behaviour and tendencies are determined by their biological history as animals. The unusual relationship shared by Oedipus and Jocasta has been considered as universal by Freud and he asserts that such tendencies are represented cryptically in dreams. The tragic hero not only lends to Freud a mythic model for sexual desire in sons for their mother but also endorses the fact that such cravings are very common to occur in dreams. The mother and wife of Oedipus Jocasta in the Sophoclean version, confronts him when he gets agitated with the prophecy, pronouncing that he is likely to share a bed with his mother saying —

> As to your mother's marriage bed—don't fear it.
> Before this, in dreams too, as well as oracles,
> Many a man has lain with his own mother.
> But he to whom such things are nothing bears
> His life most easily. (Sophocles 980)

The ubiquitousness of Oedipal dreams draws his attention to his own self-analysis about which he wrote to Wilhelm Fliess on October 15, 1897.

> I have found love of the mother and jealousy of the father in my own case too, and now believe it to be a general phenomenon of early childhood … If that is the case, the gripping power of *Oedipus Rex* becomes intelligible. The Greek myth seizes on a compulsion which everyone recognizes because he has felt faces of it in himself. Every member of the audience was once a budding Oedipus in phantasy, and this dream-fulfilment played out in reality causes everyone to recoil in horror, with the full measure of repression which separates his infantile from his present state. (Freud 223–224)

This helps him to justify his search for rationalised elucidation of the phenomena. Freud explains that the myth of Oedipus is "nothing more or less a wish-fulfilment – the fulfilment of the wish of our childhood" (Freud 161). He gives a detailed account of the clinical changes witnessed by a child during its development years, which is very important to illustrate to get an idea of Oedipus complex. Freud claims that there are certain instincts with which all human beings are born, i.e., the natural tendencies with which they try to satiate their biological necessity of food, shelter, and warmth. This fulfilment of the basic needs also serves as a cause of pleasure, which Freud mentions to be 'sexual'. An infant thus experiences an inherent pleasure while sucking its mother's breast, and at this point, the child gets the first glimmer of sexuality. The erotogenic zone which the child discovers at this stage is further reawakened in his adulthood while kissing or thumb-sucking. A sexual drive develops when the child intimately interacts with the mother, upon whom he is dependent, but when this drive is ripped off its basic role as a mere biological impulse, a relative autonomy is achieved.

Freud next draws our attention to the other erotogenic zones, which develop during the early stages of childhood – the oral stage mainly predominated by the drive to 'incorporate' substances through the mouth; second comes the anal stage in which the anus emerges to be the erotogenic zone. During this stage, a child derives amusement in defecation, though such measures are considered to be 'sadistic' by Freud as the child enjoys getting involved in expulsion and destructive activities. The child at this point of time also develops the habit of retaining and also learns to have a possessive control as in case of 'granting' or 'withholding' the faeces. The third stage, i.e., the phallic stage, is associated with the sexual drive, having the focus on the genitals. It is very important to note that Freud introduces the stage as 'phallic', which seems to be patriarchal to the later critics, mainly to the feminists as only the male organ finds its mention in this context. Freud further makes it clear that the stages do not follow a strict order; rather they often overlap and are highly flexible, substituting one another, unlike the biological instincts, as their occurrences are mostly accidental and unprecedented. This disables the child from desiring a stable object for a long time; it gets entrapped and diverged, having no centre of identity and the boundaries between itself and the external world seem to get inseparable and undistinguished. The child, according to Freud, gets 'anarchic', 'sadistic', 'aggressive', 'self-involved', and 'remorselessly pleasure-seeking', being totally trapped by 'pleasure-principle'. Surprisingly, it even cannot distinguish between masculine and feminine and thus remains ungendered, though it is directed by sexual drives.

At the centre of the Freudian theory of psychosexual development in a child, lies the subject of 'Oedipus Complex', which develops during the phallic stage. Between the age of three and five, a boy seems to develop a sexual desire for his mother unconsciously, but soon realises that he cannot get driven by this urge as he sees that the father tends to get the mother's sexual attention, thereby resulting in envy and rivalry within the child. He fantasizes about challenging his father although he is perfectly aware of the fact that such feud is impossible in reality as he has both love and concern for him. At the same time, he tends to develop castration anxiety; he fears of getting castrated by his father if he discovers his covetous feeling towards his mother and thus he begets a series of defence-mechanism with which he represses his incestuous feelings, relegating them to the unconscious. Freud defines the unconscious to be a part of mind, construed by the repressed thoughts, which are too painful to reside in the consciousness. It is somewhat blurred and porous and lies outside the consciousness. The child finally finds an idol in his father and identifies with the role of a patriarch since the repression and sublimation processes, which are at play in the unconscious, are mainly governed by the 'law of transformation'; in the concept of Freud, it is the re-channelling of those drives or impulses that are unable to gain an admissible outlet.

Freud's concept of the human psyche or personality helps to get a clear idea of the connection between childhood experience and adult behaviour. In his personality theory (1923), the human psyche is viewed as a tripartite structure, consisting of the 'id', the 'ego' and the 'superego'. They do not have a physical existence, but a theoretical function. The id forms the primitive and instinctive component of the human mind that only exists from birth. Being the only source of all psychic energy, its response to the instincts is quite spontaneous. All the aggressive and sexual drives including the hidden memories constitute this part of the personality. Apart from that, it encompasses the inherited biological drives – 'Eros', the sex instinct, which is associated with the libido, sexual desire, or energy and 'Thanatos', the death instinct, which is stubborn and aggressive by nature. Unaffected by any kind of reality or logic, it only reacts to the pleasure-principle and operates within the subconscious fragment of the mind. When the id meets with its demands, urges, needs, and desires, it provides joy and satisfaction, but if it fails to achieve its requirements, it results into immediate irritation, displeasure, or tension, disregarding its repercussions. The id is thus selfish, wishful, illogical, irrational, and fantasy-oriented aspect of the human personality. In complete contrast to the id, the superego incorporates the voice of conscience and aids in self-criticism. It gets highly influenced by the moral code of the society and hence is completely aware of the ethical and moral conduct of the community. A number of restrictions are issued during the phallic stage, i.e., three to five years, when the superego mostly dominates and this forbids the infant to submit itself to its sex drives and aggressions. The superego also functions in persuading the ego to undertake a moralistic and ethical approach and in turn insists to strive for perfection. It consists of two mechanisms – 'conscience', which penalises the ego through guilt feeling and 'ideal self' or 'ego-ideal', which imparts the social code of conduct. The third component of the human persona is the ego, which only constitutes the conscious personality. Being the decision-making faculty of the personality, it tries to strike a perfect balance between the actual reality and the unreasonable, chaotic, and fanciful id. Unlike the id being driven by the pleasure principle, ego operates through reality principle, working often rationally to satisfy the demands of the id and sometimes denying the pleasure or gratification to escape from any unwanted scenario. It follows the social norms and etiquette, while guiding the conduct and behaviour of the subject. It also seeks pleasure and satisfaction but not at the cost of affecting itself or the id. Freud considers id to be a horse and ego to be the horse rider, directing its movement towards achieving fulfilment in life.

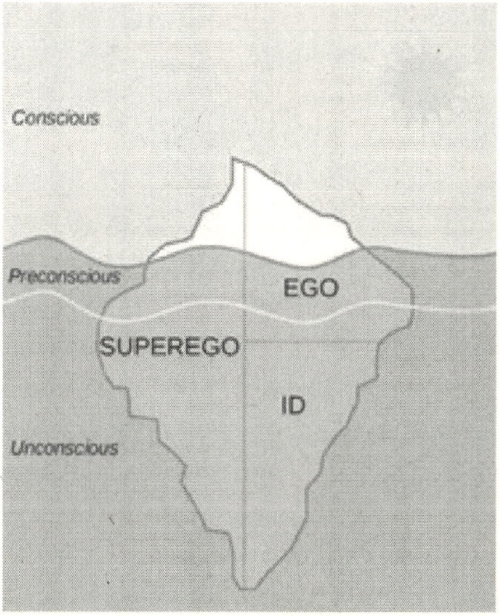

In short, ego acts as a variable aspect of the subject contrived as a system of principles or beliefs that helps to deal with the inherent quests of life based on certain rules, which Freud calls the 'secondary process'. Both the constructive and destructive biological and instinctive demands of the id are brought into harmony by the ego with the social commitments and the social constructs of the superego, along with the claims of reality. The ego helps the subject to meet with the demands of both its id and superego, without causing any destruction to itself as well as its surroundings through 'constructive acceptance' and 'laws of transformation'. Psychoanalytic therapy helps the subject to free itself from the repressed fantasies and fears in both thought and feeling by gaining access to the latent emotions and hidden feelings through 'dream interpretation' and 'transference' of attitudes and behavioural patterns onto the analysts, which are meant to be directed towards the parents. According to Freud, lost memories, linguistic symbols, repressed experience, and 'anarchic' materials being inherited often serve as the sources of dreams, which Freud describes to be the wish fulfilments that originates from inner conflicts and tensions, having the function of allowing the subject to continue to sleep. The process of transference of demands, emerging from the unconscious, into symbolic objects, manifested in the preconscious initially and subsequently in the conscious mind, is called 'Dream-work'. On the other hand, the method by which these symbols are decoded and recovered from their hidden contents is called 'Dream Interpretation'. Freud, through this explicit theory, conveys the role of sexuality in human psyche and psychological development.

Freud's treatment of dreams varies significantly from the only surviving collection on the interpretation of incestuous dreams from classical antiquity, i.e., *Oneirocritica*, written by Artemidorus of Daldis in the late second century CE. The book reports important evidence on different attitudes toward incestuous dreams in antiquity. It has been evinced that a huge cultural chasm exists between the classical Athens and the imperial Rome and beyond to the boundaries of Vienna, yet Artemidorus pursued a long tradition of dream interpretation in the Mediterranean. "In the different cities of Greece and at great religious gatherings in that country, in Asia, in Italy and in the largest and most populous of the islands, I have patiently listened to old dreams and their consequences" (Artemidorus 1). Dream interpretations were considered to be charlatan in those days by the intellectual and elites, but Artemidorus' allegiance to the empirical and proto-scientific belief that past events help to predict future outcomes compelled him to ignore the disapprovals of his peers and carry on with his venture of interacting with even the supposed unwilling clients. He names six fundamental principles for analysing dreams, which include nature, law, custom, occupation, names, and time, whose connection with the dreamer, in accordance to the dream, is generally, though not universally, considered auspicious. He also puts forward the fact that five of these six categories are constructed by the society itself and any one may have more significance than nature, which for agreeing more with a restrictive category, may cause greater consequence than for disagreeing more with a general category. He establishes his argument with an example of a potter dreaming of beating his mother, which is considered to be auspicious surprisingly as it connotes an impending profit. Here, the mother does not indicate his biological mother, rather it symbolises Mother Earth, the universal mother. A potter by occupation beats the earth and hence his professional role seems to gain more prominence than the universal implication of beating one's own mother. For Artemidorus, mother figures have symbolic entity, often referring to the country, state, or nature. "The case of one's mother is both complex and manifold and admits of many different interpretations—a thing not all dream interpreters have realized." (Artemidorus 79)

Artemidorus recognises and conforms to the holistic and synchronous estimation of the self, acknowledged in both Hellenistic philosophy and medical thought, where nature and society seem to reiterate the fundamental facets of psychological construction and vice-versa. He concludes that a dream-like human psychology tends to align with the various roles that the subject plays in the society. The fear arising from the archetypical dream of anxiety is commonly defined by the dreamer's social identity. Critics discover a flaw in this Artemidoran theory, asserting that he never specifies the reason behind the very existence of different dream visions in the dreamers, having various experiences. The most frightening dream even appears to have a positive implication. According to his logic, even the vision of beheading indicates that the person on trial would escape the event. In complete contrast to this, Freud designates that society and nature representing sexual drive seems to be in constant struggle with one another, which recapitulates Plato's classical model, exclaiming that soul and body constantly contest with each other for supremacy. He further states that society puts several constraints upon the natural impulses, thereby permitting only specific forms of sexual expressions, which leads to a 'diachronic' and contradictory image of the self, as illustrated in the human psyche as the ego and id.

Latest studies have tried to identify the fundamental theoretical difference between the two dream interpreters – Artemidorus and Freud. S.F.R. Price in 1986 clearly stated that the basic tenets of their theories are poles apart from one another and hence any comparison between the two would be meaningless. The topic of sexual desire is far more explicitly and elaborately dealt by Artemidorus' dreamers than that of Freud's patients. Oedipus complex can never be considered to be the only response to the first sexual encounter in childhood, which forms the basic line of thought in Freudian psychoanalytic theory. Artemidorus' dream interpretations also concern incestuous relationship between other family members, friends, slaves, animals, and gods along with the mother. Nineteenth century Vienna found some of the interpretations to be too awful to deal with in academics. Price even pointed out that the German translation of Artemidorus to which Freud referred and consulted excluded the section of sexual dreams, which was later added in a separate version. Both Roger Pack (1955) and John Winkler (1990) observed that Freud concluded from his study of Artemidorus that the *Oneirologist* only dealt with the social identity of the dreamers, completely ignoring their personalities and paying very little attention to their individual activities. Artemidorus had built his notion considering only a freeborn male to be his client and thus he was accused to be a classist, but both Pack and Winkler cited instances where he studied a wet nurse, a tax collector, a brothel keeper, and many others, who cannot be counted in any manner among the elite class. Christine Walde have admitted the fact that the "dream phenomena itself" (Walde 130) have considerably changed from the second to the twentieth century. Artemidorus opined that many dreams help to anticipate future occurring, while Freud presumed that most dreams serve the purpose of revelation of the dreamer's internal character. On various points, thus they have significantly differed from one another, yet they certainly share some common aspects of the method of dealing with their clients and patients.

A very common term of the twentieth century 'Lacanianism' refers to the study and development of the fundamental ideas and concepts of the eminent French psychoanalyst Jacques Lacan. The theory of Lacanianism started as an analysis of Freudian hypothesis, but eventually evolved into a new psychoanalytic notion of mankind, gaining worldwide acclamation. In the second half of the twentieth century, Lacan gave a structuralist interpretation to the Freudian concept. His concepts of condensation and displacement are corresponded to two basic poles of language, which the linguist Roman Jakobson identified as 'metaphor' and 'metonymy'. While developing the stages of human psyche, he begins with the pre-oedipal stage in a child's life, which ends in six months. During this early stage, the child suffers from a chaotic mix of perceptions, needs, and feelings. It remains undistinguished from its parents and the external world around and thus exists closest to its mother, being one with the mother's body. He calls this stage to be 'Imaginary' (pre-oedipal) and describes this idealized identification with the mother. He mentions about the child's psyche and the environment it resides in, using terms like 'innenwelt' and 'unwelt' respectively, being identified as a random, fragmented, and shapeless indistinguishable mass.

Between six and eight months, the child learns to distinguish between the 'self' and the 'other'; Lacan calls it the 'mirror stage'. In the formulation of this stage, he draws upon Heidegger's notion of 'existence' and 'nothingness' and Sartre's concept of distinguishing the subject from the ego as formulated in his concept, "Transcendence of Ego". At this stage of its formative years, the child looks at the mirror and discovers its own image in it. For the first time, he identifies himself as a separate entity and dissociates itself from the world around it. This idea tends to echo Freudian stage of primary narcissism. It falls in love with its own reflection and this love supersedes its love for all others. A sense of unified self is achieved at the cost of this self, considered to be as the other, i.e., the mirror stage. Defining it in term of structuralism, the child is the signifier and the image is the signified; the child assigns meaning to itself. The ego originates during this moment of alienation, when the child gets fascinated by its own reflection. The ego is thus constituted and shaped by the organising and constituting features of the image. The illusion of the wholeness of the body and the misperception of having complete ownership of it gives birth to this ego, which helps the child to sustain its misconception (méconnaissance). The child at this stage continuously denies the reality of its being fragmented and alienated. Unfortunately, despite of this delusion and continuous refusal of the reality, the ego remains in a state of harmony and discord; it becomes a site of continuous struggle and conflict, which Lacan refers to as a 'lack of being', i.e., a lack of desire, well manipulated by consumer capitalism. It is the ontological gap or the primary loss at the core of subjectivity, which is at play, but both Deleuze and Guattari critiqued the concept in *Anti Oedipus: Capitalism and Schizophrenia*.

> Lacan's admirable theory of desire appears to us to have two poles: one related to "the object small a" as a desiring-machine, which defines desire in terms of a real production, thus going beyond both any idea of need and any idea of fantasy; and the other related to the 'great Other' as a signifier, which reintroduces certain notions of lack.
> (Deleuze and Guattari 27)

The desire mentioned here is not 'a pure desire' for identity, but "a desire to obtain absolute difference" (Lacan b 276). Deleuze and Guattari, the two schizoanalysts, developed their concept of 'desiring machine', similar to this Lacanian hypothesis. Like Lacan, they also pondered upon the urge to discharge or liberate from its fixation on primary objects. They all shared the same impulse to liberate desire to a relief that signifies no lack or impossibility and is not measured by pleasure as it is what distributes intensities of pleasures and restricts them from being suffused by anxiety, shame, and guilt. It is humbly admitted that a wish to escape from desire may not always guarantee a happy ending. Any process of liberation involves conservation as well as destruction, and there is equal possibility of encountering both joyous consequences and terrible outcome, which may overturn the line of flight into a line of death and thus be death driven. Human behaviour is hence determined by the repression of desire or, in other words, the unconscious.

The next stage being the 'symbolic stage', based on which Julia Kristeva conceptualized the notion of 'semiotic', is the time when the child steps into the language system, which is mainly concerned with isolation and lack, though there is no existence of names at this stage; a linguistic sign substitutes it. Language and desire are in turn linked with each other. In Écrits, it has been explained in details:

> The human individual sets out with a particular organism, with certain biological needs, which are satisfied by certain objects. What effect does the acquisition of language have on these needs? All speech is demand; it presupposes the Other to whom it is addressed, whose very signifiers it takes over in its formulation. By the same token, that which comes from the Other is treated not so much as a particular satisfaction of a need, but rather as a response to an appeal, a gift, a token of love. There is no adequation between the need and the demand that conveys it; indeed, it is the gap between them that constitutes desire, at once particular like the first and absolute like the second. Desire (fundamentally in the singular) is a perpetual effect of symbolic articulation. It is not an appetite; it is essentially excentric [sic] and insatiable. That is why Lacan coordinates it not with the object that would seem to satisfy it, but with the object that causes it … (Lacan a viii)

The child begins to socialize with the external world in this stage but it faces various hindrance and provisions in the form of a patriarch, the father figure, which seems to disrupt the narcissistic balance between the mother and the child.

The phallus for Lacan is not a mere male genital organ rather a privileged signifier, which activates the whole process of signification. This process involves three stages – the imaginary, the symbolic, and the real, where the difference between the symbolic and imaginary orders has been analogous to the distinction between the small 'other' and the big 'Other', often considered to be its corollary. In the imaginary order of the middle stage, the little 'other' emerges as the reflection or projection of the child's ego in the guise of ideal 'I', which further appears to be its own counterpart and represents the other person or entity in which the child seeks its visual likeness or specular image of its own body. On the other hand, the symbolic order incorporates the big 'Other' being identified as a radical alternate, which perpetuates the fallacious and deceiving otherness of the imaginary, not being able to get recognition through identification. This alterity is often associated with law and language by Lacan. The other becomes the other subject or the symbolic order, which helps intercede with the other subject. If this hypothesis is to be applied to the domain of literature, it can be concluded that the most realistic literature most importantly features the world of patriarchal order and logic, whereas in case of an anti-realistic literature, the realms of imaginary get prominence; language signifies objects beyond itself as well as beyond logic and the text itself. The same distinction between the imaginary and the symbolic order corresponds to the contrast that exists between poetry and prose. Lacan appears to have a preference for a literary text, where the imaginary continuously shows a tendency of erupting into the symbolic as in case of 'metafiction' or 'magic realism'; the novel negates its only realism and narratives.

The last stage in Lacanian psychic structure is the 'real', that denotes to the world which exists before the mediation of language. It can never be comprehended in totality, rather an attempt is continually made to grasp or engage with it through the imaginary and the symbolic. Thus, to incorporate language, the child has to expose itself to the inevitability of desire. As language pronounces the 'fullness' of the imaginary, fragmenting it into small pieces, it also cuts the subject from the 'Real', i.e., beyond the symbolic order.

In the words of Lacan,

> The 'real' emerges as a third term, linked to the symbolic and the imaginary: it stands for what is neither symbolic nor imaginary, and remains foreclosed from the analytic experience, which is an experience of speech. What is prior to the assumption of the symbolic, the real in its 'raw' state (in the case of the subject, for instance, the organism and its biological needs), may only be supposed, it is an algebraic x. This Lacanian concept of the 'real' is not to be confused with reality, which is perfectly knowable … (Lacan a ix)

An offshoot of psychoanalytic theory is 'Object Relations Theory'. The theorists of this concept assume that the psychological birth happens in an individual through his or her social relations with other people around him or her. It extends over the first three years of life, which are characterized by a symbiotic relationship to his or her primary caretakers, especially the mother, followed by his or her separation from the caretaker, and finally a stage of individuation, when different skills or personal traits are established in the individual. The determination of gender occurs within the first eighteen to twenty-four months. In this line of criticism, gendering of the subject is not at all associated with the child's awareness of sexuality and reproduction, which is completely in contrast to Freudian or Lacanian hypothesis, yet any kind of injustice in the value associated with the gender, is imbibed along with the corresponding disparity in power. This development of the persona in the infant culminates through the process of reciprocation of the responses to the needs and desires of the other. Thus, from one to six or seven months, very similar to Lacan's imaginary stage, the infant hardly can sense any kind of distinction between itself and the caretaker, and hence remains very sensitive to the moods and emotions of the caregiver, especially its mother. The mother needs to be always emotionally available to the child, remain conflict-free herself, and must restrain from developing a narcissistic overinvestment of her own self in the infant in order not to allow any kind of hostility and resentment to arouse within her by the infant's desire. She also at the same time needs help from other people around her to help her maintain her own sense of autonomy.

When the child is around six months age, it begins to develop a sense of separation which continues through the second year, giving rise to both pleasure and frustration at the same time as it gets aware of its own limitations. Jane Flax argues that –

> The child explores and continually develops its separateness, then returns to the mother for 'emotional refueling'. The potential presence of the relationship between child and mother allows the child to leave it. Gradually the relationship is internalized and becomes part of the child's internal psychic reality. Both members of the dyad must learn to let go of the early bond without rejecting the other. The ambivalence present throughout this process gradually intensifies. The child both wants to return to the symbiotic state and fears being engulfed by it. In 'good enough' social relations a resolution is achieved in which both members of the dyad come to accept their bond (mutuality) and their separateness. This is the basis of a truly reciprocal relationship with others. (Flax 252)

The process of developing 'self-identity' and 'gender identity' is a very complex process for children. In the initial stage, their identity remains fused with that of their mothers, and hence, both boys and girls consider their gender to be that of their mothers that is necessarily feminine. Eventually as they grow up, the boys have to repress their symbiotic experience along with the feminine traits of their nature by continually denying their identification with their mothers and by blaming women for being the source of the problem through the process of domination.

> These defences become part of ordinary male behavior toward adult women and to anything which seems similar to them or under their (potential) control – the body, feelings, nature. The ability to control (and to be in control) becomes both a need and a symbol of masculinity. Relations are turned into contest[s] for power. Aggression is mobilized to distance oneself from the object and then to overpower it. The girl, on the other hand, seeks relationships, even at the expense of her own autonomy. The two genders thus come to complement each other in a rather grotesque symmetry. (Flax 253)

At this point of time, they strongly identify with their fathers, thereby developing a strong self-identity but a weak gender-identity. The fathers cannot offer a viable alternative of the symbiotic mother and so in case of girls they form a weak self-identity but a strong and less troublesome gender-identity. The key insight of the Object Relations theory thus conveys that human subject is socially determined being the product of social interaction and its nature is highly shaped by the social relation between the subject and its caretakers.

Freudian psychoanalytic hypothesis has been considered flawed by many contemporaries including Melanie Klein, Luce Irigaray, and others, due to its inadequate conceptualization of the women psyche. Melanie Klein's theory of the conscious shares much of its major concepts with the Object Relations School of theory, considered to be a variation of psychoanalytic theory, which focuses more on the interpersonal relationships of an infant than the biological sexual drives like the 'id'. Klein considers the mother-child relation to be central, rather than the father-child one. According to her, the infants get exposed to certain anxieties in their phantasy life from birth while feeding and they start to treat the people they come in contact with as objects and part-objects. To them the term 'objects' does not refer to any inanimate entities, rather it indicates their mother, father, or to their primary caregivers. These infantile fantasies are the psychic representation of the unconscious id, which has no connection with the conscious fantasies of their adulthood.

Being the member of the Berlin Psychoanalytic Society, Klein observed that the young children often manifest their anxieties or aggressive fantasies regarding the part-objects of their parents – the breast, the penis, the unborn babies in their mother's womb, or their own play objects like toys or on their drawings, thus acting out their desire for reparation through role play. On getting a chance of expressing, they get a chance of getting rid of their anxiety.

The first four to six months after birth is called paranoid-schizoid position by Klein, when the child is rooted in primal fantasy. According to Freud, the basic biological drives of the child are generated by 'Eros', i.e., the 'Life Instinct', but for Klein, it is the 'Death Instinct', which is at play. Freud has completely ignored this particular faculty. Klein explains that the ego takes its shape immediately after the infant is born; the new-born child perceives the whole world through part-objects. The mother, who is considered to be its prime object, gets reduced to a part-object, i.e., the breast of the mother.

Klein next attempts to introduce the process of splitting. This occurs when a person, mainly a child, fails to cope with two contradictory emotions at the same time and therefore chooses one to rely upon.

> Central to object relations theory is the notion of splitting, which can be described as the mental separation of objects into "good" and "bad" parts and the subsequent repression of the "bad," or anxiety-provoking, aspects (Klein a 145)

The child experiences this very process of splitting for the first time with its primary caregiver, i.e., its parents, especially the mother. When she can successfully satiate its demands, she is considered to be good or otherwise bad. The infant naturally encounters with a lot of anxiety, emerging from various traumas after birth, hunger, frustration etc. It tends to split the mother's breast into 'Good' (when it satisfies its hunger) and 'Bad' (when it provides any kind of restrictions). Splitting thus acts as a defence mechanism, safeguarding it from undesirable and detrimental emotions and feelings. In Klein's words –

> The Ego is incapable of splitting the object – internal and external – without a corresponding splitting taking place within the Ego ... The more sadism prevails in the process of incorporating the object, and the more the object is felt to be in pieces, the more the Ego is in danger of being split. (Klein b 19)

The infant practically consumes the good part-object by ingesting the mother's milk, which to the baby, gets projected as a symbol of love and life instinct, but at the same time, the hunger pain together with its own aggression regulates the 'Bad Breast' within its body and tries to save the 'Good Breast' from it. 'Projection' and 'Introjection' are two unconscious processes of splitting, which control the paranoid anxieties, both internally and externally. Klein here echoes the concept of Freud, asserting that both optimistic and pessimistic fervours are projected or casted by infants upon external objects, which continue in their adulthood in the form of hatred and fear, often leading to racism, war, and genocide. Often people have a tendency of extracting and focusing on the positive attributes, ignoring the negative ones in order to feel happy and secure. This process of 'Projection' is further culminated into the mechanism of 'Projective Identification', which involves the fantasy of projecting a part of the subject itself into the other person or object in place of the unwanted split-off 'part-objects'. This approach involves a blurring of the boundaries, which cannot be seen in case of 'Projection'. Since a part or rather an extension of the infant is projected into the mother (object), the child considers in his omnipotent fantasy that it can have full control over it and can manipulate it accordingly. It tries to pass on its own frustration to its mother. Wilfred Bion's notion of countertransference is credited for inspiring Klein's concept of Projective Identification, though she never approved it as a theory; she instead accused it for having its utilisation only in therapeutical purpose. The psychoanalytic theory of counter-transference enables the therapist to transfer their unresolved conflicts onto that patient and hence this method seems to be quite dangerous.

The Paranoid-Schizoid Position is followed by the 'Depressive Position', which occurs in the baby's first year, though its first manifestation can be observed in its weaning stage, i.e., in around three to six months of age, when a child first learns to respond to the reality and tries to secure a place for itself in it. The infant experiences loss and mourning due to its first separation from the mother, which includes the loss of its narcissistic fantasy, where it considers its ego to be the whole world and mourns the loss of the objects, which it has hurt or attacked or damaged through aggression and jealousy. It feels guilty first and then a drive for love and reparation arises from its guilt conscience. During this time, a child perceives the world in a new way. The defence mechanisms such as splitting, introjection, or projection is no longer required; the infant can have a more accurate idea of the inner and outer world. The whole persons are no more considered to be part-object and the child can realise others' feelings and emotions. Absence is no more a persecutory attack, rather a loss, and anger is replaced by grief. It first arises in its real tears in this stage. It is interesting to know that Klein designates the two states of mind to be 'positions' instead of 'stages' as they do not follow one another; rather the infant is found to oscillate between the two during its development years.

In a lecture in 1924, Melanie Klein talks about Oedipus complex for the first time but she extends Freudian ideas and gives a new guise to the old oedipal situation as described by Freud. She assumes the fantasies of an infant prefiguring a horrifying parent couple – the maternal body with a male penis and rival babies, exhibiting sadistic oral, utheral, and anal features due to the functioning of infantile sexuality and sadism. This fantasizing of the maternal body leads to the inducing of primary femininity as well as to the male and female Oedipus complexes.

Freud considers the super-ego of an infant to be a positive development, but to Klein, it is a hostile superego, which gets generated in the oral stage. The ambivalent awareness of the whole object along with the depressive guilt for infantile aggression compels the subject to renounce the oedipal desires, permitting the internal parents to come together. Klein challenges the supremacy of the male oedipal complex by asserting that penis envy is more of a defence against a larger primordial fear of getting attacked from either parent as incorporated in the infantile superego.

Similarly, Luce Irigaray, a prominent interdisciplinary thinker of the twentieth century, was a student of the famous analyst Lacan, but she strongly criticized the whole psychoanalytical theory as developed by Freud, Lacan, and others, due to its exclusion of women from a genuine social existence of being an autonomous subject and thus earned fame as a feminist and continental philosopher. She has written a series of critical texts, providing a comprehensive analysis and critique of the Freudian and Lacanian philosophy, thereby arguing that they have failed to realise that female subjectivity cannot be apprehended through the lenses of a one-sex model. She started her criticism with her famous critical work, *Speculum of the Other Woman* (1974).

Irigaray asserts that traditionally women have been considered analogous to nature and unthinkable matters. Women since ancient times have been designated the role of a mother, whether she is actually a mother or not, such that her identity remains defined only by that role, which is completely in contrast to the men being associated with culture and subjectivity. Women are thus the unrecognised support of men and are never acknowledged as full subject, yet society fails to function without their share of contribution. The entire Western society and culture is based on the sacrifice of women through the role of a mother. According to her, sexual difference does not exist since otherwise it requires men and women to be equally considered agents of subjectivity, but in the

Psychoanalytic School of Criticism, men are considered to be subjects like self-conscious and or self-same entities, while women are designated as 'the other' of these subjects, i.e., the non-subjective supporting matter. In Western philosophy, there is only one form of subjectivity that exists, i.e., the men, while women are the inert, lifeless, and defunct part of the society. Irigaray aims to formulate how women must start to reconstruct their own identity such that one sex ceases to exist at the cost of another, but she does not want to hint or prescribe any particular form of the new identity; rather women should find this for themselves.

The discipline of psychoanalysis plays a unique role in supporting philosophy as a discourse. There is no doubt that philosophy alone cannot be blamed for the history of female subjugation, yet similar kind of ignorance can be observed in both the discourses. Irigaray credited psychoanalysis for its method of analysis, which helped to reveal the plight of female subjectivity, but according to her, it forcefully controls it. Freud and his fellow analysts tried to analyse female sexuality and subjectivity following the male model, but they failed to realise that they have projected a negative connotation to the nature of women through their theory due to their practical bias. Women, according to Irigaray, must achieve subjectivity and reconstruct their own identity and men at the same time must be much more embodied. This will help both the sex to comprehend that they both belong equally to nature and culture. She gave special attention to this fact while commenting on various subjects and dealing with different themes, which include mimesis, novel language and utopian ideals, mother-daughter equation, alteration of language itself, ethics, and politics.

Irigaray's philosophy of rejecting the universal male symbolic order so as to project sexual difference is considered to be the 'radical feminist' phase of the feminist movement. Her famous work *An Ethics of Sexual Difference* opens with the assertion that each age is characterized by a major philosophical issue; her time has been mainly defined by sexual difference. Her engagement with psychoanalysis and linguistics mainly unveil the lack of a valid sexual difference in the Western context. She, while critiquing Freudian psychoanalysis, defined the speculum in *Speculum of the Other Woman* and *This Sex Which is Not One* as a curved mirror of feminine self-examination, as opposed to the flat mirror, privileging the relation between men, thereby ignoring completely the feminine. She always rebelled against the 'law of sameness' that works within all discourses. Men and women are being repeatedly merged into one single entity, highlighting that man is the measure of all thing, a famous claim made by Protagoras of Abdera, a fifth century Greek philosopher, which is completely refuted by Irigaray. She exclaimed that the whole Freudian theory of sexuality is premised on one sex, i.e., the male; there is mention of the male and, on the other side, there is the absence or the 'lack'; i.e., the female. Freud has considered male to be the paradigm of all sexuality, including both the physical changes and the sexual pleasure. Sexuality for Freud is thus a 'priori male'. She further accused Freud of discussing vividly about the 'lack' of 'Phallus' (a Lacanian term) in females, while completely overlooking the degeneration of breasts in the males, which should also be deemed as 'a lack' in males. She even blames Lacan's failure in recognising the error of his predecessor Freud as he himself formulated a master signifier of the Symbolic order, the Phallus, which is again a projection of the male body, though Lacan himself denied of having any connection to the male autonomy. In *Cosi Fan Tutti* (*This Sex Which is Not One*), she affirms that Lacanian concept of Phallus is nothing but an extension or rather a reinforcement of Freudian construction of one-sex model, which is used as a tool to describe the whole world and hence Phallus as a master signifier evince the fact that the Symbolic order is a mere human construction and nothing more than being ahistorical.

Freud's lack of distinct attention to the female sexuality came into the notice of Carl Jung along with Melanie Klein, Luce Irigaray, and others. It is not that Freud never mentioned about female psychoanalysis, but he has described its functioning in terms of male psychoanalysis. This had dissatisfied Jung and he coined the term "Electra Complex" in 1913, deriving the name from the mythological character of Electra, who with her brother Orestes, avenges the murder of their father by plotting against their mother. Freud never approved of the concept and accused it as an unnecessary attempt to emphasize the analogy between the attitudes of the two sexes.

The character of Electra and her tale is recounted in several versions by ancient authors like Aeschylus, Euripides, Sophocles, and others. Both the playwrights Euripides and Sophocles have written their own version of the narrative in 5th century BCE, but there has always been confusion among the classicists regarding the fact whether Euripides or Sophocles was the first to give the myth a literary shape. Both the versions considerably differ from each other, though the backdrop remained almost the same.

Euripides' version of the 420 BCE story, narrated that Electra, although being the love object of a number of royal suitors, has been thrown out of the royal family by being married off to a poor farmer in order to prevent her beget children of high status as they might avenge the death of Agamemnon. Her husband, a peasant of Mycenae, is very kind and loving. On the other hand, Orestes, Electra's brother, has been sent to the king of Phoeis by their mother Clytemnestra to keep him away after his father's death. He develops a close friendship with the king's son Pylades, and after they grow up, they both decide that they will disguise as strangers and go to Electra to make sure of her loyalty towards their father. Though Electra does not recognise his exiled brother, yet she invites them and reveals her sad story in front of them. The old servant who accompanied Orestes has been able to recognise him easily from an old scar on his brow and thus both the siblings get reunited. They decide to take revenge of their father's unnatural death and thus make a plan. Electra sends words to Clytemnestra that a baby is born to her and so she wishes her to come and bless the baby, while Orestes confronts Aegisthus hunting and kills him with the help of Pylades. When they both bring his body to Electra's house, she convinces Orestes that he needs to kill Clytemnestra also give justice to Agamemnon. When Clytemnestra arrives, he thrusts a sword into her and thus fulfils his duty.

The play ends with Castor and Pollux, the brothers of Clytemnestra, appearing and warning them that matricide is considered to be a shameful act and so both the siblings must cleanse their souls, thereby following their instruction. Electra must marry Pylades and renounce her husband's home and Orestes will be chased by the Furies and must suffer the fate as decided in the trial.

Euripides also wrote another play *Orestes*, which can be considered to be a sequel to the earlier one. It begins with a soliloquy of Electra, while standing next to the sleeping Orestes, detailing the series of events that have taken place in the past. Helen visits to make an offering to her sister Clytemnestra. She is followed by a chorus of Argive women, who help to advance the plot.

Orestes awakes getting agitated by the Furies and discusses his condition with Menelaus, his uncle, but he is too spineless to provide any kind of assistance. On the other hand, the citizens of Argos plan to put Orestes, Electra, and Pylades to death for their crime along with Helen, whom they held responsible for the Trojan War. They also decide to abduct Helen's innocent daughter. This would result in a total chaos in the city. At the end of the play, peace gets restored by the *deus ex machine*, who prevents the upcoming chaos of violence and the attempted murder.

Sophocles also in around 400 BCE used the same background in his version of the narrative. King Agamemnon of Mycenae also known as

Argos in some versions of the myth has just come back after the Trojan War, accompanied by his new concubine Cassandra, which aggravated the grudge borne in his wife Clytemnestra against him for many years since he has sacrificed Iphigenia, their daughter, at the beginning of the Trojan War to satisfy the Gods. By then Clytemnestra has already chosen Aegisthus, Agamemnon's cousin, as her lover and plots with him to kill both Agamemnon and Cassandra. They have sent Orestes, Clytemnestra and Agamemnon's son, to Phocis to keep him safe, while their daughters Electra and Chrysothemis continue to stay in Mycenae almost with the status of a servant. After a few years, Orestes returns as a grown man with his friend Pylades, son of Strophius and a pedagogue. To gain access in Clytemnestra's palace, they spread a rumour that Orestes is dead and, in guise of two strangers, Orestes and Pylades arrive to deliver an urn with his remains. Electra meanwhile grieves over Agamemnon's cruel murder and her inability to avoid staying with his murderers. She clearly displays disgusts and hatred for her mother and informs her sister Chrysothemis that she can never forgive her involvement with the murder. She only hopes that one day Orestes will return to take the revenge of the father's death. On hearing the news of Orestes's death, Electra gets shattered but Clytemnestra feels relieved. Chrysothemis surprisingly notices some offerings of flowers and a lock of hair at their father's tomb and suspects that Orestes must have returned, though Electra refuses to believe her. Rather, she proposes that in her brother's absence it is their responsibilities to avenge their father's murderers, but Chrysothemis declines her plan, considering it to be impractical.

When the disguised Orestes hands over his urn to Electra, which is supposed to be containing his own ashes, she breaks down in despair. Seeing her in bitter emotion, Orestes gets emotional and reveals his own identity, thereby displaying their father's ring as a proof. Soon, the siblings get overjoyed being reunited after such a long period of time. Immediately, they hatch a plan to murder Clytemnestra before Aegisthus returns. The plan gets executed as it has been decided but when Orestes comes to inform about his success to Electra, who has been waiting outside to keep a watch, they find Aegisthus approaching. Aegisthus, on meeting Electra, asks her for the Phocians, who have brought the news of Orestes's death and she points inside the palace. He orders to open the doors and gates so that the citizens can have a look at his corpse, but Orestes brings Clytemnestra's body in its place. Aegisthus gets worried discovering Clytemnestra's corpse, realising that he too will be murdered soon. The play ends with Orestes instructing to take Aegisthus to the same spot where he kills Agamemnon as, according to him, it is the appropriate place to a avenge his father's death by murdering Aegisthus there.

In the 5th century BCE, probably Aeschylus was the first to pen down a trilogy named *The Oresteia*, concerning the Electra narrative with a few variations from the later versions. The three parts of the trilogy include *Agamemnon*, *The Libation Bearers*, and *The Eumenides*. The plays were originally performed in Athens during the Dionysian festival, where it secured the first position. A satyr play *Proteus* was originally included along with the trilogy, which was supposedly based on Homer's *Odyssey*, but nothing except a single line of it still exists.

The first play of the trilogy *Agamemnon* narrates the homecoming of the King of Mycenae Agamemnon from the Trojan War, while his wife awaits to avenge the sacrifice of their daughter Iphigenia and to overcome the forthcoming hindrance in the path of her lordship and finally to embrace Aegisthus as her lover. Aegisthus also has a grudge against Agamemnon since his father Thyestes has been tricked by Agamemnon's father Atreus earlier into consuming his own two sons and so he has nurtured the desire to exact the revenge on Agamemnon. The plot progresses with Agamemnon being stabbed to death, followed by his concubine Cassandra's death and finally the return of the exiled Aegisthus.

In the next play *The Libation Bearers*, Orestes, the son of Clytemnestra and Agamemnon, returns with his cousin Pylades to seek revenge of their father's assassination following Apollo's order. He meets her sister Electra at their father's grave, where they plan their further course of action. The second play is also called by the name of *Choephoroi*.

The last play *The Eumenides* ends the trilogy with the tormenting trio of the Goddess of Justice known by the name of the Furies, who relentlessly keeps pursuing Orestes for committing matricide. Orestes has been able to escape them for a short while they fall asleep but Clytemnestra's ghost wakes them up. He seeks shelter from Goddess Athena and pleads her to save him. Heeding to his request, Athena arranges a mock trial with twelve Athenian citizens under her own supervision and declares that her vote will decide his final fate. She determines that Orestes will not receive death but the Furies strongly oppose her. Athena finally convinces them by giving them a new name 'Eumenides', meaning 'the kindly ones'. She gives her final verdict stating that no further cases will be settled personally; rather all trials must be carried out in court.

There is a lost play named *Electra* written by Quintus Tullius Cicero, though nothing much is known about it except its name and it was a Greek tragedy written in the classical Greek style.

In all the versions of the story of Electra, she has played the primary role of being the agent, who has brought about the tragedy by instigating her brother Orestes to kill their mother in order to give justice to her dead father's murderer. It has been noticed in a few versions that Orestes refuses to commit the murder, but he cannot escape the constant pressure of his sister. This role of Electra gives hint to C.G. Jung about the orientation of female sexuality, which was never given prominence separately in the male-dominated social structure. Edmund Leach, while pondering upon Levis Strauss's analysis of the Oedipus myth as explored in the Greek mythology, opined that it "is simple enough: if society is to go on, daughters must be disloyal to their parents and sons must destroy [replace] their fathers" (Leach 83). His opinion gives a clear hint that parents first had been socially reduced to 'fathers' followed by inverting generation and cross-sex relationship. Women were under the control of their fathers, brothers, husbands, and their own grown-up sons in the ancient Greece. In order to maintain their domination, men had not thought twice to bind their daughters or sisters and at the same time attempted to displace their sons as well, which explains the mechanism of inverting generation and cross-sex relationship. Freud's version of Oedipus complex had been theorised from the perspective of Oedipus, his affiliation towards his mother, and displacement of father. There has been no effort made to analyse the female psyche, giving no attention to the role of Antigone, the daughter of Oedipus, or Electra, the daughter of Agamemnon, whose roles are no less than heroes in the Greek mythologies. Their heroism could have been explored much extensively not only in literature but also in psychoanalytic theory.

Homeric odes clearly evince the fact that women were consistently subordinate and submissive to men in the classical society as he deliberately excluded the episode of Electra and the matricide committed after the murder of Agamemnon. According to the Homeric order, it is a man and not a woman, who gets involved in blood revenge, and so it is Aegisthus in his version, who kills Agamemnon and succeeds him as a king. On the other hand, Orestes takes vengeance on Aegisthus but orders for a grave mound for both Clytemnestra and Aegisthus. In *Odyssey*, Homer characterizes Clytemnestra as an utterly wicked, shameless, and a monstrous wife of Agamemnon, who in absence of her husband, exercises political power. In the Homeric world, women were taken to be "naturally inferior … limited … to the production of offspring and ... household duties" (Finley 138). Cassandra in contrast is presented as a pitiful victim of Clytemnestra in both Homer and Aeschylus's version, and in her words, the character of Clytemnestra is depicted as –

> She is the lioness, she is the savagery,
> when the lion's away she's the bed-company
> kept by the skulking jackal... does nobody see?
> Her potion's made: one ingredient's death for me.
> And hear this She boast, as she whets the knife for her He,
> that death is the price of his triumph's including me.
> So why stand to be laughed at in clothes of prophecy,
> in Apollo's necklace, with staff of augury? (Aeschylus a 31)

She continues –

> What's the right name to give to a monster like her?
> Two-headed serpent, vampire of the coasts
> coaxing the ships she's hexed onto wrecking reefs,
> the raging mother of hell exhaling war
> on all her kin, the bitch whose triumph-howl—
> all-daring as the male-most warrior's—
> showed her ambiguous joy at his return ... (Aeschylus a 32)

Until the nineteenth century, there had always been a tendency to either deify a woman character or to cast them as demons in literature, which is also well evinced in the classical texts. Clytemnestra in all the versions of Aeschylus, Euripides, and Sophocles although being cheated by her husband, emerges as a strong character, which perhaps is the sole reason for her to get landed as a victim of matricide. Athena, a marital goddess born of Zeus's head, herself gives validation to male domination in the version of Aeschylus by helping Orestes to get absolved from the crime of matricide. She justifies her final judgement, thereby advocating for the male supremacy stating –

> There was no mother who brought me to birth;
> I take the male side in everything,
> excepting marriage; I'm my father's child.
> And so I will not give the precedence
> to the death of a wife over the man she killed,
> the lord and overseer of the house.
> And if the votes are equal, Orestes wins. (Aeschylus b 25)

Even Apollo, who charges Orestes of killing his mother, puts forward the Greek law of procreation –

> To what we call her child, the natural mother
> is no true parent, but a fosterer.
> The parent is the one who plants it there,
> the male who spurts his seed within her womb;
> all she does, like a host who feeds a guest,
> is grow his seedling in her—if god wills. (Aeschylus b 22)

Despite of having all the heroic traits, Clytemnestra never enjoys the status of a hero in any of the versions of the narrative purely because of her gender. The wronged wife and mother, wielding an axe, has always received the portrait of a monster, having only the Erinyes (the female monsters) or the Furies as her avengers, but unfortunately their powerful resistance also gets overruled by a virgin goddess, who is herself deprived of a mother's womb.

Electra, the daughter of Clytemnestra and Agamemnon, has a contrasting reception. She gets a chance to enjoy the heroic stature in her own right. Aeschylus's version delineates her conventionally as a weak and indecisive woman. She only appears in the first part of the play when she is sent to pour libations on her father's tomb. She gets confused not knowing what to do and is thus advised and guided by the chorus. They remind her to include her brother Orestes in her prayer. Her position is no better than a slave in the house and she even laments the fact that both her brother and she have been sold by her mother to purchase Aegisthus. Even while the siblings join each other to invoke Agamemnon, Electra wishes to remain more temperate of heart than her mother. She does not contribute either in making the plan for the murder or in the execution of the plan of avenging their father's death.

In contrast, Euripides introduces Electra in his version primarily to force Orestes to commit matricide. Her presence is extremely necessary for Orestes to avenge his father's death on his mother and her lover. Electra for Orestes is more of a mother-substitute than being a mere sister. Sophocles' version of Electra is a much stronger and self-determined character, who "resolve to act, that rock against which the waves of threat and prosecution will break in vain" (Knox 10) in the public mourning of her father and even appeals to him to be revenged. She further grieves that had she not been a virgin, she would beget a son to avenge her father's unusual death, but according to her, she is past the child bearing stage. She complains of getting abused, starved, and tortured in the hands of both her mother and Aegisthus, whom she hates and fears as she has been confined to their house by Aegisthus for long. She has a sister Chrysothemis, who unlike her, remains in peace instead of suffering in a similar way as she has yield to the authority. Electra can never submit herself to the kingship of Aegisthus and so when she gets informed that her brother Orestes for whom she has waited so long is dead, she resolves to slay Aegisthus all alone with her own hand as she has been denied by her sister when she asked for her help. If that would be the case, Electra perhaps would be disqualified as a hero as taking blood revenge is considered to be stepping outside the feminine role, but she has been saved by the revelation that Orestes is still alive and is abetting the vengeance.

It is quite evident that Sophocles' Electra is equivalent to Antigone from many perspectives. C.G. Jung formulated Electra as the female equivalent of Oedipus and tried to metaphorically symbolise a daughter's feelings towards her parents, but Electra in none of the version has committed incest with her father and she was always deprived of the presence of her father, initially due to the war and later due to the unusual death on his return. Both Antigone and Electra were bereft of their mother's love and attention. While Antigone's mother has killed herself by self-inflicted violence, Electra compels her brother to slay her mother. They both have a loving relation with their father. Both Antigone and Electra have to remain unmarried and childless for the sake of their fathers; Antigone has to support her blind father, while Electra has never been married by Clytemnestra and Aegisthus, though many royal suitors have wished to take her. The two women were likewise represented as heroes, being deprived of their mothers' love, attention, and care; they became bound to their fathers and sacrificed their marriage and motherhood for their sake. Jung views that a metaphoric father-daughter incest can be responsible for the victimising of woman as it leads to appropriating and dedicating the life space of her for the father (brother), which otherwise would have been devoted to her husband and children. The women as heroes can never play the role of wives and mothers at the same time. Antigone and Electra are thus heroic but deprived women.

Carl Jung excludes the brother figure in his version of the Electra myth. According to his reading, jealousy emerged as an earlier feature as compared to sexuality and hence he concluded that "with budding eroticism" (Jung 154), a son develops the Oedipus complex for his mother, while a daughter develops an Electra complex. Jung's expansion of Freud's Oedipus complex in 1913 through his own theory of Electra complex is oversimplified as an intention to portray the female version of the Oedipus complex, but in actuality, he develops the theory to fill the theoretical vacuum, which he noticed in the Freudian theory.

Jung started with his opinion that a girl is much more emotionally attached or bonded with her mother in the first three years of her life as compared to a boy. This initial bond will be again observed in her later stages as 'the return', when she will feel a need to identify with her mother to internalize a few maternal trials into her personality, thereby accommodating her mortality in the 'superego'. A sudden change occurs in the next one year, i.e., at the age of three or four years, when the love object shifts from the mother to the father, upon realising the 'lack' in her, and thus her new approach towards the father leads to an unusual rivalry and distancing from the mother. She seems to grow jealous and exhibit possessiveness for the father and even feel hostile upon getting denied of some objects from a father figure. At six or seven years of age, she returns to her mother and begins to feel the same closeness with her as her initial days. She often imitates her and gets curious of the feminine role, thus stepping into the feminine world and realising her gender role. Jung views this phase to be responsible for constructing her emotional, social, and psychological behaviour, which will further mature along with time. So, the Electra(s) of the Greek tragedies are found to be mourning for the father, trying to escape the deprived condition, getting clung to the brother, supporting the brother in his vengeance, and even at times, attempting to convince her brother to avenge, but in none of the cases, she herself murders her mother. The Jungian version of the Electra myth ultimately justifies the feminist critiques of the psychoanalytic theory, which advocates the universality of Freudian Oedipus Complex and the necessity of the pre-Oedipal mother, who is the mother of a baby from its dependent infancy to personality development. The feminist Freudian theory always maintains that the pre-Oedipal mother continues to remain intact in a growing girl, resulting in the attachment between daughter and mother to persist forever.

The feminist critical theories of psychoanalysis give very little importance to Jung as, according to them, his hypothesis of female psychic development can put an end to both the motherhood and society. They opine that if, according to Jungian representation, Electra would murder her mother with her own hand, she would have to remain as an outcast, isolated, and polluted human being throughout her entire life as the Greek society never permitted such a girl to survive in a healthy state. Aeschylus' Electra is seen to be an obedient daughter of her mother, while Sophocles' Electra hates her primarily not because of losing her father due to her but perhaps mainly because of the abuse or deprivation, she has to suffer for her. It has also been evinced that Euripides' Electra would have killed her own self had Orestes failed to avenge Aegisthus. In fact, she is later seen to lament for the murder of her mother. Jung, on the contrary, suggests that the Electra myth works as a destructive force and aids in bringing the tragic fate in the whole family. The Sophoclean version of Electra, even after being unloved and revengeful, has sacrificed her marriage and motherhood for her brother Orestes, who "takes the place for her simultaneously of son, father and husband" (Vernant 143).

All the characters in the classical Greek narratives – Oedipus, Antigone, Electra, and Clytemnestra, through their paradigmatic myths, give insight to child psychology. The term 'paradigm' is a Greek word, which literally means pattern or demonstration. Sophocles' Oedipus is addressed as a paradigm in *Oedipus the King* – "a demonstration ... that man's keenest sight is blindness, his highest knowledge ignorance" (Knox 145). Sigmund Freud took the clue, taking into account the figure of Oedipus as a paradigm, to construct a paradigm of childhood development, but he had missed to notice the mythic women in the Greek literature, where there are illustrations of their relation to their fathers and brothers as well as to their husbands and sons. Both Antigone and Electra in the Sophoclean tragedies are paradigms of a woman as a hero and victim. They surely show their heroism by transcending the conventional feminine roles, but they are careful enough not to deny or violate their gender roles. They emerge as victims of their own heroism. Clytemnestra, unlike the two, reverses the gender roles and proves herself to be an exception.

This universality of the Freudian concept of Oedipus Complex, which he conceptualised while interpreting the Oedipus myth, is critiqued by Malinowski, who found it to be corresponding to the European family only; further asserting that "the nuclear complex the European family and that "the nuclear complex of the family ... must vary with the constitution of the family" (Malinowski 4). Malinowski identifies power struggle instead of sexual jealousy to be the driving force behind oedipal complex in non-Western societies. Anne Parson applies the idea of the issues of nurture and matrilineal societies along with sex and repression of Malinowski's theory to the Southern Italian society and the Mediterranean world. While doing her fieldwork in Naples, she presents several data, which includes the Madonna of boundless love and forgiveness; the daughter's virginity considered to be a part of her father and brother's honour; the greater importance being given to the mother than the father in the family; the significance of the association of the male members of the family with the other men outside the family etc. In doing so, she identified a third nuclear family complex apart from the Freudian Oedipus Complex and Malinowski's matrilineal variant, which is characterized by the man's emotional dependence on his mother, father and son's antagonistic relationships, or the relationship shared by the female or women members in the family with their brothers or fathers, in which incestuous impulses are seen to be more dominant than the Oedipus Complex. Parson's illustration of the prominence of the Southern Italian mothers in the family in her 'Nuclear Complex' theory helps to recall the submissive domestic roles of husbands and fathers as compared to wives or the mothers in the ancient Greece. The Greek mythologies have always focused on the role of daughters in case of women rather than their roles as wives or mothers and hence, the paradigmatic heroic women figures like Sophocles' Antigone and Electra could not become wives or mothers.

Many facets of these theories related to the psychosexual development in a child have been argued to be established with minimal evidence in practical life and thus it becomes difficult to delineate them as universal phenomenon, without considering various social and cultural factors. Many critics even denied of having any scientific evidence of these hypotheses as the predictions made by these theories are not substantiated by experiments. So, being counted among the most prominent developments of the twentieth century, fascinating several critics, both the Oedipus complex and the Electra complex got their prominent manifestations in the field of literature.

A parallel theory in the field of psychoanalysis had been developed by the anthropologist Edvard Westermarck. Westermarck strongly opposed Freud's concept of the family members developing lust for one another naturally, thereby accusing it for instigating the society to create incest taboos. He argued that taboos are created naturally as outcomes of a simple inherited epigenetic response, i.e., from non-genetic effect or gene expression. The Westermarck effect can be defined as a hypothetical psychic development through which people living in close proximity in the early years of a child's life gets desensitized to later sexual attraction in its adulthood. Westermarck postulated through his theory that physical proximity can be used as a kinship cue to avoid incestuous relationships. Despite of this reverse sexual imprinting, the literary critics of the twentieth century and the authors of all ages have neither discarded the Freudian Oedipal theory nor the Jungian Electra Complex theory totally. Several literary texts in the history of English literature are found to be exploring these psychoanalytic theories as their major themes and thus gaining the attention of several literary scholars and readers for years.

Works Cited

Aeschylus, a. *Agamemnon*. Translated by Timothy Chappell, https://www.gutenberg.org/files/14417/14417-h/14417-h.htm. Accessed 22 May. 2022.

———. b. *Eumenides (The kindly ones)*. Translated by Timothy Chappell, https://www.ancient-literature.com/greece_aeschylus_eumenides.html. Accessed 22 May. 2022.

Anon. *The Thebaid.* qtd. in https://www.newworldencyclopedia.org/entry/oedipus. Accessed 18 May. 2022.

Artemidorus. *The Interpretation of Dreams (Oneirocritica)*. Translated and Edited by Robert J. White, 2nd ed., Original Books, 1990.

Deleuze, Gilles and Félix Guattari. *Anti-Oedipus: Capitalism and Schizophrenia.* University of Minnesota Press, 1972.

Finley, M. I. *The World of Odysseus*. Viking Press, 1954.

Flax, Jane. "Political Philosophy and the Patriarchal Unconscious: A Psychoanalytic Perspective on Epistemology and Metaphysics." *Discovering Reality*, Edited by John Symons, University of Texas, 2003.

Freud, Sigmund. a. *The Complete Letters of Sigmund Freud to Wilhelm Fliess 1887-1904.* Translated and Edited by Jeffrey Maoussaieff Masson, The Belknap Press of Harvard University Press, 1985.

———. b. *The Interpretation of Dreams.* General Press, 2019.

———. c. qtd. in "Id, Ego, and Superego". https://www.simplypsychology.org/psyche.html. Accessed 19 May. 2022.

Hesiod. *Theogony And Works and Day*s. Translated by M.L. West, Oxford University Press, 1988.

Jung, C.G. *Freud and Psychoanalysis. Collected Works, Vol. 4.* Pantheon, 1961.

Klein, M. a. *The Psychoanalysis of Children*. W W Norton & Co., 1932.

———. b. "Notes on Some Schizoid Mechanisms". *Projective identification: The fate of a concept*, edited by Elizabeth Spillius and Edna O'Shaughnessy, Routledge: 2012.

Knox, Bernard M.W. *The Heroic Temper: Studies in Sophoclean Tragedy.* University of California Press, 1964.

Lacan, Jacques. a. Écrits*: The First Complete Edition in English.* Translated by Bruce Fink, Héloïse Fink, Russell Grigg, W.W. Norton & Company, 2006

———. b. *The Seminar. Book XI. The Four Fundamental Concepts of Psychoanalysis.* Translated by Alan Sheridan, Hogarth Press and Institute of Psycho-Analysis, 1977.

Leach, Edmund. *Claude Levi-Strauss*. Viking, 1970.

Malinowski, Bronislaw. *Sex and Repression in Savage Society.* Kegan Paul, Trench, & Trubner, 1927.

Pindar. *Pindarπs Victory Song.* Translated by Frank J. Nisetich, Johns Hopkins 1980. https://web.as.miami.edu/personal/corax/pindar.html. Accessed 19 May. 2022.

Sophocles. *Sophocles I: Oedipus the King, Oedipus at Colonus, Antigone.* Translated and Edited by David Grene, Richmond Alexander Lattimore and Elizabeth Wyckoff, University of Chicago Press, 1954.

Vernant, Jean-Pierre. *The Forest of Symbols: Aspects of Ndembu Ritual.* Cornell University Press, 1967.

Walde, Christine. "Dream Interpretation in a Prosperous Age? Artemidorus, the Greek Interpreter of Dreams." *Dream Cultures: Explorations in the Comparative History of Dreaming.* Edited by D. Shulman and G. Strousma, Oxford University Press, 1999.

III

The Mother Archetypes: Great Mother and Terrible Mother

Greek literature has not only featured the most controversial and most frequently visited theme of parent-child rivalry, but the Homeric hymns in particular have also provided us instances of mothers' sincere devotion to her children. The narrative of Demeter and Persephone forms a ripe example of a mother's overbearing and over-possessive love for her progeny. Persephone, also known by the name of Kore or ko'ree ('girl' or 'maiden'), is the daughter of Zeus and Demeter. One day, she goes to pluck flowers, being accompanied by the daughters of Ocean, where, at the will of Zeus and to content Hades, Earth produces a radiant and magnificent narcissus, which naturally draws the attention of Persephone. As she reaches to pick the flower, the Earth yawns and Hades appears in a golden chariot and carries her away against Persephone's wish or will. She shouts for help and calls out to Zeus but he turns a deaf ear to her. It has been his plan to give his daughter to Hades (Pluto), his brother and Persephone's uncle, in marriage to be the queen of the underworld. Demeter has been completely ignorant of this plan of Zeus. On hearing the frantic screams of Persephone, she rushes in pursuit but in vain. In rage, she refuses to consume ambrosia or drink nectar and even she has not bathed for nine days; she has only roamed around the world with burning torches in her hands with a heavy heart. Hecate hears her howl but feels helpless not being able to reveal the truth. On the tenth day, when the Sun-God Helius can bear no more of her pain, he divulges the truth on one condition that she shall not lament. He tries to console her stating that Hades will be a good husband to her daughter as he is a great God, who has been made the king of the underworld when the divine power gets divided into three ways. Instead of giving any comfort, the news intensifies her grief and she gets furious with Zeus as according to her he is the one responsible for her daughter's rape. She conceals her beautiful appearance and begins wandering among the mortals in disguise of an old woman. She also starts avoiding and ignoring the Gods on Olympus. After roaming for a few days, she reaches Eleusis, where she sits beside the Maiden Well just when the wife of Celeus, the king of Eleusis, and his four daughters come there to draw water. There they notice Demeter in her disguised form and begins questioning her about her identity. She makes up a story; she tells them that her name is Doso and she is abducted by some pirates from Crete, from whom she has somehow escaped when they disembarked. She also tells them that this land is unknown to her and so she pleads them to find her some work as a housekeeper or a nurse. Callidice, the prettiest daughter of Celeus, upon seeing the pitiable condition of the old woman, feels sympathetic towards her and asks her to wait there until she returns after seeking permission from her mother.

Metaneira, the wife of Celeus, has given birth to her only son a few days ago. Hearing about Doso, she immediately instructs her daughters to hire her as a nurse at any cost. Doso comes in a dark robe with a veil covering her head. As she steps into the threshold, her head touches the beams and the doorway gets lit up with a divine radiance, which amazes Metaneira. She requests her guest to be seated on a splendid couch, but Doso refuses and waits until a servant brings a decorated chair with a fleece over it. She even denies accepting any food or drink offered to her, although to observe the holy rite, she asks her to mix the meal with water and mint, which she consumes. She starts taking utmost care of the baby and gives her full attention always. She even begins to develop motherly love for the boy and so she decides to make him immortal by burying Demophoön within the blazing fire, but one day Metaneira spots the immortalizing process and being terrified starts to scream. This enrages Demeter and she stops the process immediately. Nevertheless, since the boy has slept in her arms, she allows him to flourish as a mortal with imperishable honour along with instructing Metaneira for the future of Eleusis, proclaiming that "I am Demeter, esteemed and honoured as the greatest benefit and joy to mortals and immortals," (Homer 239). Then she casts off her old look and regains her actual size and appearance. A divine radiance and an unusually pleasant fragrant air surround her as her golden hair flows upon her shoulder. With this she disappears, leaving Metaneira overcome by shock and fear. Before leaving the palace, she also instructs the citizens of Eleusis to construct a great temple as well as an alter beneath the town on the rising hill on the top of the well Kallichoron, where she vows to teach them her rites, with which they can satiate her heart. King Celeus obeys her instructions with full dedication.

Demeter after leaving Demophoön, whom she treats as a substitute for her daughter for a short while, continues to grieve and as a mark of fulmination she makes the whole year disastrous for the mortals, thereby giving no harvest; the Earth has not borne a single sprout. This petrifies the Gods because if this continues for a longer time, famine is a certainty. The future of the whole human race is at stake. The Olympian Gods will also not receive any offerings, gifts, or honours from the mortals if the mankind perishes, which seriously worries them. Zeus ultimately can no longer stay unmoved. He has to send Iris to the Eleusian temple, where Demeter has been residing, with a request to join the company of Gods. Demeter instantly declines the plea. Zeus, refusing to give up, begins sending all the immortal Gods one after another with gifts of her choice to convince Demeter, but all goes in vain. She refuses to step into Olympus unless she sees her daughter with her own eyes again. Having no other option, Zeus has been forced to send Hermes to Hades in the underworld to explain all that has happened and to seek permission to bring Persephone with him so as to save the mortal world from Demeter's wrath. Hades, listening to the entire story, immediately obeys Zeus's order with a smile and gives instruction to return Persephone to her loving mother. At the same time, he wishes to convey the message to Demeter that he has never been an unworthy husband to Persephone as, being the full brother of Zeus, he always allows Persephone to rule the underworld as the Queen being a great Goddess. In her kingdom, if anyone refuses to propitiate her power by not performing holy rites and declines to give offerings to satisfy her, he is bound to find eternal retribution.

Persephone gets overjoyed to get such an instruction and jumps out in the happiness, but secretly Hades gives her a pomegranate to eat as a symbol of remembrance of her husband's order that she will not stay with her mother forever, rather she will also return to him to rule the underworld for some time of every year. He then hitches his immortal horses to a golden chariot on which Persephone immediately mounts. Hermes takes the reins and instantly they are in front of Demeter's temple.

Demeter, on getting the glimpse of her daughter, rushes out with the passion of a maenad and they both welcome each other with their arms around each other's neck. But soon she can sense some deception, and to confirm, she asks her whether she has consumed any fruit from the underworld. When Persephone spills out the truth, Demeter informs her that she can live with her for two-third part of the year, but for the rest one-third part of the year, she has to spend in the underground. With the burgeoning spring, she will return to the upper world every year. Persephone continues to describe in details how, against her will, Hades has taken her to the underworld and later tricks her into eating the pomegranate before her return. The grave and agonising situation soon turns joyous with a longer and tender embrace. Hecate at the very moment suddenly arrives and shares the joy and so from then onwards, she has been appointed as one of the attendants of Persephone.

Zeus next sends Rhea to bring Demeter back into the Olympian world among the Goddess and he also promises to allow Demeter to have her daughter for two-third part of every year along with all other honours that she chooses to have. This time Demeter complies with his wish and in turn also restores the fertility to the human world, saving them from further starvation. The whole world again blooms with flowers and fruits miraculously.

Before returning to the Olympian Mountain, she fulfils her promise, which she has made to the Eleusian people. She teaches the leaders of the place how to perform the sacred rites and preaches them about the holy mysteries, but she has also made them vow not to violate, question, or reveal any of these to anyone. After ordaining all that she has decided to, she happily returns to the world of Gods with her daughter ultimately. They have also sent Plutus, the God of agricultural plenty, prosperity, and wealth, to their beloved mortals, who has served Demeter for so long. The hymn ends with proclaiming that the mortals, who have witnessed all these occurrences, are happy in their lives and the ones, who have not been able to take part, are also destined to a similar joy after their death in the gloomy realm in the underworld.

The story of Demeter and Persephone is often believed to be a symbolic representation of the seasons of a year. Persephone's separation with her mother causes the earth to wither and die and hence it is claimed to be the autumn and the winter season. On the other hand, Persephone's reunion with her mother causes the earth to rejuvenate, bringing new hope of fertility and so it represents the spring and the summer seasons.

Demeter-Persephone myth has been interpreted differently by 20th century and early 21st century critics. In this context, Jung explains that a woman lives first as a daughter and later as a mother. By losing Persephone, Demeter lost her own maidenhood and Persephone lost her first love object, with whom she identified, in getting separated from her mother.

Persephone is also known by the name of Kore and the three-fold narrative of Demeter-Kore cycle has many psychophysical implications, as first noticed and mentioned by Carl Gustav Jung, which mainly focus on issues like mother-daughter identity, development crisis, adolescent emancipation and detachment, erotic triangulation, sexual initiation etc. Jung comments in this context that Gods have emerged to become diseases; Kore can be considered to be a ubiquitous eating disorder, while Demeter being the hallmark of maternal role-boundedness, enmeshment, poignancy, and cycling despair. The physical severance and emotional disconnection with the daughter can only be held by the reunion of transformation that will help to restore the maternal psyche.

The tale of the abduction of Persephone followed by her resurrection and subsequent return initiates a mystery religion at the meadows in Eleusis, most commonly known for the frequent rape cases that occurred and devastated the lives of the common people there. This myth however continues to give hopes to the Egyptian initiators of getting a promising life after death for establishing the cult. These initiates being exposed to the major motifs of the myths include pristine virginity, deception, rape, lust, abduction, frustration, and reunion of a mother and daughter, experiences a profound spiritual transformation, that never allowed them to spill out the secret rites concerning the cult, which they vowed to keep it to themselves. Jung suggested that this narrative has not only opened an avenue to philosophical speculation, but also at the same time has initiated to produce a psychedelic brew termed as the 'kykeon' (light), which provoked a visionary experience known as 'epoptia', and the glittering vessel, in which the kykeon is served, symbolises the body of light. The child residing within every female spirit must overcome the fear of being unconscious, thereby emerging as the queen of the feminine empowerment.

Demeter, the earthiest variant of the Mediterranean Great Goddess, not only symbolises fertility, but also the boon of agriculture given to the ancient Greeks. She represents the fertile and cultivated soil, while her daughter Persephone is considered to be the virgin soil. The shift from the main occupation of hunting to cultivation marks a dramatic metamorphosis in the history of early civilizations. Persephone in the form of Kore or Virgin personifies the inner divine child of the feminine psyche, one part of which resides in the light, while the other half in the dark subconscious. It is through this inner child that all of us are exposed to the external harsh world and are subjected to unknown fears, which we are unaware of and also often fail to recognise and thus get entrapped and raped by life, but we are expected to overcome it all by ourselves without waiting for any external assistance.

> In Greek mythology, a term for the personification of feminine innocence (e.g., Persephone); psychologically, in man or woman, it refers to an archetypal image of potential renewal. The phenomenology

> of the Kore is essentially bipolar (as is that of any archetype), associated with the mother-maiden dyad. When observed in the products of a woman's unconscious, it is an image of the supraordinate personality or self. In a man, the Kore is an aspect of the anima and partakes in all the symbolism attached this inner personality.
>
> As a matter of practical observation, the Kore often appears in woman as an unknown young girl … The maiden's helplessness exposes her to all sorts of dangers, for instance of being devoured by reptiles or ritually slaughtered like a beast of sacrifice. Often there are bloody, cruel, and even obscene orgies to which the innocent child falls victim. Sometimes it is a true nekyia, a descent into Hades and a quest for the "treasure hard to attain," occasionally connected with orgiastic sexual rites or offerings of menstrual blood to the moon. Oddly enough, the various tortures and obscenities are carried out by an "Earth Mother." ... The maiden who crops up in case histories differs not inconsiderably from the vaguely flower-like Kore in that the modern figure is more sharply delineated and not nearly so "unconscious." (Jung 185)
>
> Demeter and Kore, mother and daughter, extend the feminine consciousness both upwards and downwards. They add an "older and younger," "stronger and weaker" dimension to it and widen out the narrowly limited conscious mind bound in space and time, giving it intimations of a greater and more comprehensive personality which has a share in the eternal course of things … We could therefore say that every mother contains her daughter in herself and every daughter her mother, and that every woman extends backwards into her mother and forwards into her daughter … The conscious experience of these ties produces the feeling that her life is spread out over generations-the first step towards the immediate experience and conviction of being outside time, which brings with it a fe*eling of immortality.* (Jung 188)

Demeter, being an earth-mother, very similar to the Greek progenitor Gaia, seems to get represented physically as the seed (Persephone), transplanted underground, which is a form of abduction to the underworld, returns to the surface of the Earth in the spring when the grain starts sprouting. The mythological figure of Demeter in actuality functions to symbolise much more than a mere agricultural metaphor. Similarly, in the myth recounting the rape of Persephone by Hades, Persephone's relationship with Hades and her stay in the underground denotes the fallow winter, which spans for one-third part of every year. Apart from that, it also indicates the phenomenon that all mortals sleep or rather remains unconscious for one-third part of every day. This Persephone (conscience) that lies within us is dragged every day under the surface of the earth (conscious or psychic world) deep down beyond the threshold of consciousness into the profound realm of the unconscious. It is commonly believed that sleep is a temporary death, while death is a permanent sleep. Dreams on the other hand emerge from the perspective of the soul or the psyche rather than that of the ego. Hades' empire of darkness symbolising death can also serve to be a metaphor of the man's instinctive memories and servitude to the collective part of the human race. Besides being the emperor of the underworld, Hades seems to rule over the unconscious province of the human psyche.

Persephone due to her marriage gets hitched to this state of human consciousness thereby getting entrapped into a new state of identification. She transforms from a virgin maiden (Demeter's daughter) to Hades' austere wife and queen of the domain of the underworld. Psyche was given the task of robbing some of Persephone's beauty, which can be interpreted as a means of seeking the beauty of death in order to ease out some of the pain of grief and bereavement or, separating one from his active life; death being considered to be a counterpart of birth and life force, complementing each other. Psyche's shamanic tour to the domain of the underworld anticipates the probability or possibility of a later resurrection or rebirth. In real human life, this descent to the underworld may transpire through the death of a family member or any closed one, which will result in sucking the person into the dark sphere of the underworld. This further leads to an instinctive or compulsory retreat or withdrawal from the people around. The other different pretexts which may lead one to such a condition can be grief, betrayal, physical molestation, depression, or addiction. Chemical addiction can also be a reason which compels one to congress with the criminal world as a form of the underworld, but this union unlike the other types is socially disgraceful. Psyche characteristically seems to become suicidal having suffered so deeply and this underworld remains as an immortal realm. It is a challenge for the victim at this state to remain conscious and aware of the agonising experience.

The history of the Eleusinian mysteries, taught by Demeter to the people of Eleusis along with the rites and the cultivation of wheat, conveys two categories of initiations – one concerned with reunion of man with the Gods, while the other points out to the possibility of man to achieve immortalization. This enlightens the aspirants to free themselves from the subconscious fears by overpowering them in order to achieve blissful existence after death. Mircea Eliade describes how the death (abduction) of Persephone has considerably affected mankind, asserting – "As the result of it, an Olympian and benevolent goddess temporarily inhabited the kingdom of the dead. She had annulled the unbridgeable distance between Hades and Olympus. Mediatrix between the two divine worlds, she could thereafter intervene in the destiny of mortals." (Eliade) The celebration of the cult continued for the next two thousand years as the archaeologist could discover the footprints from the place, where they danced around the well, making grooves in the stones. Due to the various social and cultural changes, the rituals have undergone various alterations later, though the implication remains the same. Psychologically, though depression feels like death, it is expected that the sufferer must bear it with tolerance just as Persephone has embraced the feeling of alienation, passively enduring it, and deepening it even further. The depressed victim is seen to get transfixed by the power of death, making it difficult for him or her to resist the grip, but it is only by being one with the mystery and by undergoing the shamanic initiation that it implies, he or she can escape the negative evaluation of the 'underworld' experience and be at home even in the underworld.

On the other hand, Demeter's pathology, being extremely grieved and mourning carelessly the suffering of separation, has exhausted all her life-giving and nurturing energy. Her sense of loss felt like loss of her own self, which further becomes self-indulgent, being unable to control. This rage of a mother can actually harm and wound her own children. Her animus, being enslaved by patriarchy, could not protect her own progeny. She herself could not free her own self from the father-complex and so also failed to keep her child safe from this ravaging masculine force. Deliberately, she had to wear a mask of self-control, of perfectionism, and of idealisation of family roles; although being passively aggressive, she had to feign to appear docile because of being exposed to the severe repression.

The Demeter and Persephone myth acts as a lens according to the Arrien Angel to speak of the isolation and fear of family betrayal, and the various means necessary for working through loss to regain the lost dignity and recompense with the expression and reception of the family affliction in *Nine Muses: A Mythological Path to Creativity* (2000). This initiated to weave tapestries of reconciliation and renewal. The myth of Demeter and

Persephone at the same time forms a ripe example for a psychic condition known by the name of "Borderline Personality". Christine Ann Lawson, in her book *Understanding the Borderline Mother: Helping her Children Transcend the Intense, Unpredictable and Volatile Relationship*, asserts – "Children who grow up with borderline mothers live in a make-believe world that is neither fiction nor fantasy. Borderland is an emotional world where loving mothers resemble storybook characters." (Lawson 4) There is hardly any existence of boundaries, while the emotions are also often repressed and sometimes even they are too heavy to cope up with and this puzzles the children of borderline mothers as they cannot be sure of which actions of theirs incite praise and which will offend them. It is never clear to such children of borderline parent as to how they should behave or react in front of their mothers in particular as the slightest infringement may cause them to be irrevocably exiled from their mother's heart and attention. To be precise, in Lawson's words, "children in Borderland are puzzled by the contradictions of their world and live on the fine line between sanity and insanity" (Lawson 5) or between the rich harvest and the dark underworld, i.e., the land of death and decay. Demeter as predicted by Lawson can be considered to be an instance of borderline mother, who are generally prone to suffer some major loss in her childhood or may have faced some kind of neglect as a child. Demeter had a motherless upbringing and could not thus experience her own childhood, being captivated in her father's belly until Zeus, her brother and later husband, rescued her along with her other siblings. She longed to relive and enjoy her lost childhood days, which she always craved for, through her daughter. She had also missed the mother-daughter bond, normal to every child, being separated from her for such a long period of time. This made her to grow to be an overbearing and over-possessive mother to her progeny. She sought for all her gone happiness, her emotional stability, and her entire existence in her daughter, and thus often failed to realise the undue stress she lays upon Persephone, which may often seem to be insurmountable and inescapable to her.

The greatest fear of borderline mothers is not death; rather they get terrified at the thought of facing abandonment or separation from their daughters and to prevent such consequences, Demeter gave relentless efforts to remain locked in the indistinguishable mother-daughter enmeshment. In such cases, the female progeny often feels suffocated and can hardly get to know her own self unless she begins to sever ties with her mother, but often the child fears to escape from the entangled relationship as this may trigger the darker side of her mother's errant psyche. Kimberlee Roth and Freda B. Friedman in their joint venture, *Surviving a Borderline Parent: How to Heal Your Childhood Wounds & Build Trust, Boundaries, and Self-esteem*, observed that – "Adult children raised by a parent with BPD likely have a hard time trusting their own perceptions, their own judgment, their emotions and knowing what's normal" (Roth & Friedman 271) and, to save themselves, they have to run from their borderline mothers and seek a safe shelter, which must be far away from her reach. In the myth, Persephone, being dragged down to Hades' world, might have been proven to be an ideal scenario necessary for her own well-being and development. It has been perhaps a desirable fate as she is seen to be quite adored and honoured in the underworld.

Being free from Demeter's cloying and smothering grasp, Persephone not only could emerge as the queen (master) of the dark world, but also of her own will. Demeter had perceived this attempt of individuation of Persephone with aggression and made the whole world suffer with the same coldness, darkness, or hunger, which featured her own heart at the separation of her daughter. Clinically, in the real world, children of borderline parents face severe difficulties in dealing with them, but in contrast, Persephone got an opportunity to enjoy probably the best kind of existence, prevailing between strong impermeable boundaries on one hand, while on the other hand, "learning to serve and mirror her own ego" (Lawson 262) in place of the ego of her borderline mother at the same time, thereby ascertaining her own individuality being separate from that of her mother.

In a book named *My Mother, My Self* (1977), the author Nancy Friday investigates the mother-daughter mystery as evident in the myth of Demeter and Persephone, which she interprets to be a union of semes. Demeter, being the renascent form of Persephone, evinces the fact that women experience a matrilineal bond in the continuity of generations. This matrilineal line can be traced back to one's grandmother and mother and forward in one's daughter. A woman's requisite self gets reborn in her daughter, which enables the incongruent eternal virgin-Mother to continue to exist. It is not quite the same in case of males. In the words of Helen Luke –

> There is an immense difference between the mother-son and the mother-daughter experience. ... In the natural pattern of development, the boy will feel his separateness from his mother by reason of his masculinity much sooner than the girl and will begin striving for achievement. Everywhere, however, before the twentieth century, the

> growing girl remained at home contained in the orbit of her mother until the time came for her to become a mother herself and so to reverse the role. (Luke 30)

The blood-bond that female members share in a family seems to reveal a distinct mystery of the generation from their own substance. The paradox can be witnessed clearly in the narrative of the mother-son duo Eros and Aphrodite.

The Greek Goddess Aphrodite is considered to be the Roman counterpart of the Goddess of love, sex, beauty, and fertility, Venus, though the Roman counterpart is often considered to have little symbolic significance beyond the abilities of the Greek Aphrodite, which includes victory, fertility, and prostitution. The ancient poet Hesiod recounts the unusual birth of Aphrodite in *Theogony* from the sea foam after Ouranos (Uranus) castrates Cronus (Saturn) and his blood spills on the sea. Aphrodite gets married to Hephaestus (Vulcan), but there has been neither love nor children involved in the marriage. Apart from Hephaestus, she also has Ares (Mars) as her divine lover, with whom she gets trapped by Hephaestus within a net while making love in bed. Instead of having a childless marriage, she has not remained barren as she has many children from different Gods. She has a son named Phobos (Timor), who being the personification of fear, participates in the war alongside his father Ares. The other children of Aphrodite according to the narrative are Deimos or Metus (the personification of terror), Harmonia or Concordia (the Goddess of harmony and concord), and the Erotes or Cupids (the winged love deities symbolising various love aspects, namely Rhode, Eryx, Peitho, Charites, Priapus, and Aeneas). Later, in the Ovid's version of the narrative, Aphrodite is known to give birth to Hermaphroditos by Hermes, who has emerged to be the epitome of effeminacy and androgyny. Her daughter Tyche (Fortuna) personifies luck and faith in Roman religion. The minority deity of fertility featured with an unusually large phallus named Priapus is also ascribed to be born from Aphrodite. Pausanias mistakes the Graces to be the offspring of Bacchus and Aphrodite, but more often it is credited to Zeus (Jupiter) and Eurynome. These Graces continue to be part of the retinue of Aphrodite beside Erotes and Suadela, who is the Goddess of persuasion in the world of romance, love, and seduction.

Along with the divine lovers, Aphrodite is also known for having mortal lovers, among whom Anchises and Adonis are the most well-known. She gives birth to Eryx with Butes, the Silician king, and to

Astynous with Phaethon. A prince from Dardania named Anchises, who has been an ally to Troy, has been seduced by Aphrodite in disguise of a Phrygian princess. She reveals her divine personality after nine months. They both have a son named Aeneas. She even warns Anchises to conceal their affair from the outer world to save himself from Zeus, but he fails to keep her words and thus ends up being crippled by Zeus's bolt. In the *Metamorphosis*, Aeneas is recounted to have been the founder of Rome with his divine mother's aid. Virgil credited Aeneas' son or Iulus, the king of Alba Longa, to be the ancestor of the founders of Rome, namely great leaders like Romulus and Remus as well as Gens (family) Julia, whose family has worthy descendants like Julius Caesar and Octavia (Augustus) Caesar.

Hesiod in *Theogony* claims Eros, the primitive God of love, to be the son of Chaos, but later narratives portray him to be the son of Aphrodite by Zeus, Ares, or Hermes. He has been most commonly depicted or characterised with hitting people with arrows to make them fall in love. Psyche (the Greek word meaning soul) is the youngest among the three daughters of a king. Although being a mere mortal, she has a divine appearance and the beauty of a Goddess, which has attracted the attention of the whole kingdom and even beyond. Royal princes from far of places begin visiting her palace in order to admire and worship her. They have often remarked that her beauty even surpasses the beauty of Aphrodite and this made Aphrodite envious of the simple mortal maiden. Her temples no longer have visitors and her altars get covered with cold ashes. Even the sculptors have stopped making her idol. This very fact enrages Aphrodite. She seeks help from her son Eros in great despair. She instructs him to use his power and make the shameless Psyche to fall in love with the wildest and the most applicable despicable creature, who has ever walked on earth. Unable to bear his mother's misery, Eros comes to her rescue. He agrees to do as he has been ordered, but the moment his eyes falls upon the beautiful Psyche, his own heart gets pierced by one of his own arrow and he immediately falls in love with her. He never wants to break her mother's heart with the news and so he decides to keep the fact a secret.

Meanwhile, Psyche surprisingly has been suffering from the agony that though men from different parts of the world come to admire her but no one seems to fall in love with her. They worship her beauty but marry other women. Even her two sisters, although being much less charming, have had lavish weddings with two kings. She can no longer bear her lonely days and this also causes great anxiety and distress to her parents. Finding no other way, her father decides to visit the Oracle of Delphi to seek an advice from Apollo, but the prophecy disclosed to him has been frightening and astonishing. According to Apollo's decree, Psyche has to be brought to the summit of the mountain in black clothes and left alone until the husband reserved for her, who is supposedly a winged serpent having more powers than the Gods themselves, will come to her and take her as his wife. Unwillingly, finding no other way, all bade her farewell with tears and mourning as though she is leaving to embrace death. They helplessly leave her all alone in the designated place to her own destiny, where she continues to wait for her destined husband.

Psyche starts waiting on the dark hill all alone, which terrified her and she starts crying. One night, a fresh wind of Zephyr seems to reach her and in such a manner as if she has been raised by it. Then she finds herself to be flying over the rocky hill and finally reaches a soft meadow full of flowers, where she almost gets rid of all her discomfort and torment and falls asleep. The sound of a clear stream breaks her sleep, and after opening her eyes, she finds a magnificent castle fit for Gods, which features gold columns, silver walls, and floors made of invalid precious stones. This sight awes her and what is most surprising is that she can see no one but is able to hear a voice proclaiming that the ornate house is for her. She is further asked to enter inside without fear and take a bath and she will be immediately honoured with a great dinner. She enjoys a refreshing bath and is served delicious dishes. All the time, she remains surrounded by a soft music like that of a harp accompanied by numerous choirs. She never had such an experience all through her life before. She has a premonition that her husband will surely visit her there at night and she is correct. At night, she can feel someone close to her, whispering with a sweet voice in her ears and soon all her fear vanishes. Immediately, she can sense that it is her husband, but she doubts that he can never be a monster as per the prediction; rather the one for whom she has always been craving.

The next few days Psyche enjoys the most in her life, but one thing always worries her; she has never seen her husband. The whole day she has to stay alone and thus boredom fills her heart as even her own family is not with her. She begins to miss their company and gets anxious that her family must be mourning her absence. She decides that she has to do something to end their suffering. That very night when her husband comes, she pleads him to do her a favour. She asks him to give permission to her two sisters to come and meet her at this palace so that they get ensured that she is safe and happy here and this news will also comfort her old parents. Initially, Eros, her husband, declines her request, but seeing her sad face, he agrees to her plea with the words, but at the same time, he warns him that their influences may destroy her present bliss.

The very next day, the same wind that has brought Psyche to the palace, carries her two sisters to her. Meeting one another, they greet each other with embrace and tears. The magnificent palace along with the music and the delicious meal totally surprises them. They cannot restrain themselves from getting envious and curious of Psyche's husband. They keep on insisting Psyche to disclose all about her husband, his appearance, and his occupation. Psyche answers that her husband is a young hunter, but they have not believed her as a simple hunter can never afford such a luxurious palace; he must either be a prince or a God. They start comparing their wealth with that of hers in jealousy and eventually they hatch a plan to hurt their sister. Before bidding her farewell, they alarm Psyche that her husband must be the awful serpent that the Oracle of Delphi has predicted. They further insisted that it is probably the reason why he doesn't allow her to see him since he knows that if she sees him, she will feel disgusted and leave him forever, thus implanting a seed of suspicion in her. These thoughts continue to disturb her day in and day out.

> Why doesn't he come to me in the day? Why doesn't he allow me to see him? What is his secret? Why hasn't he ever told me about his life? … He must be hiding something horrible and that is why he does not want to be seen in the daylight. I must find out. Tonight, when he falls to deep sleep, I will light a candle to see him. If he is a snake, I will kill him. Otherwise, I will turn the candle off and go happily to sleep. (Apuleius)

She ultimately makes up her mind to forget her husband's warning of not seeing his face. That very night, when her husband has been sleeping peacefully, she gathers all her courage and takes a lamp to see his face. The lights soon revealed that her husband is perhaps the most beautiful man instead of a snake. This action of hers makes her feel ashamed and immediately she falls down on her knees to thank God for blessing her with such a fortune, but while she has bent down to see his face, a drop of oil falls on the young man. He wakes up instantly in pain to find his trust broken. Without a single word, he leaves the bedroom at once. Psyche follows her husband to plead him to return but to no avail. She cannot spot him anywhere but a devastated voice speaks to her – "Love cannot live without trust." (Apuleius) Those have been his last words before flying to the dark sky. The heart-broken Psyche begins to lament in despair – "The god of love ... was my husband and I did not trust him." (Apuleius) From that day, she begins to spend her days in tears, crying for her lost husband till she decides to get him back at any cost. She thinks of looking for him at every possible place and is ready to go to any extent for convincing him to come back to her.

Unable to find any other alternative, Psyche takes resort of Aphrodite, the Goddess of love. She visits her temple to plead her to persuade her son and convince him to get back to Psyche. On the other hand, Aphrodite has not got rid of her jealousy for Psyche and still wishes to exact her revenge. She clearly informs Psyche that to get her work done, she has to accomplish three tasks to prove that she is appropriate for her son. If she fails in any of these tests, she will lose Eros forever. Having no other option, Psyche agrees to her words and follows her on a hill, where the Goddess points towards a dune of various small seeds of wheat, poppies, millets etc. and instructs her – "I want you to separate these seeds by this afternoon. If you do not, I will never let you see Eros again." (Apuleius) This causes her immense despair as it is almost impossible to separate such tiny seeds. Her eyes get filled with tears. Just at that moment, a group of ants have been passing by and they feel pity on her condition. They decide to help her execute this cruel task. They construct several dunes from the large original one, each having one king of seeds, but seeing these small dunes, Aphrodite gets enraged and punishes Psyche by making her lie on the ground without serving her any meal, while she herself rests on a soft bed and thinks that this hard work for such a long time period of time will destroy her beauty. In the meantime, she even does not allow her son to come out of the room, in which he has been lamenting Psyche's betrayal.

The next morning, Aphrodite plans to give Psyche another cruel and dangerous work. She takes her to a fountain and announces – "Can you see those black waters descending from the hill? That is River Estige, awful and abhorrent. Fill this bottle with its water." (Apuleius) Psyche, having no alternative, accepts the task but when she reaches the waterfall, she finds that the rocks of that place are so steep and slippery that only a winged creature can reach there and approach it. This time an eagle comes to her aid. It has been crossing the river with its large wings when its eyes fell upon Psyche's helpless condition. Unable to bear her pain, it takes the bottle with its beak and fills some black water in it. Psyche returns to Aphrodite with the task done, but she receives her with a cold simile, stating – "Someone helped you ... otherwise you would not have been able to perform this task by your own. I'm going to give you another chance to prove you that you are as determined as you claim to be." (Apuleius)

The third task assigned to Psyche is the most impossible one for any mortal. Aphrodite gives her a box and commands her to visit the underworld where she will find the Queen of the Dead, Persephone. She must ask her to drain a bit of her beauty in the box, which is to be brought to her. Psyche just like the earlier ones helplessly agrees to execute the order. She starts on her journey along the path that leads to Hades' realm. She reaches the gate of the underworld, where she finds the water body, which she has to cross. Charonte, the boatman, helps her to find her way to Persephone's palace. Happily, Psyche rewards him with a lot of money. When she meets Persephone, she explains her condition and the demands of Aphrodite. Hearing this, Persephone gladly drops a drain of her beauty in the box as she is happy to fulfil Aphrodite's wish. Psyche takes the box merrily and hands it over to Aphrodite, but on receiving it, instead of getting happy, she gets furious. She shouts to her that she will never give her permission to go and will always treat her as a servant.

This time, the Gods of Olympian Mountain can no longer stay quiet. They have to interfere to give justice to Psyche. They have sent Hermes as a messenger to Eros to inform him about all that Psyche had to face to get him back. Eros' wound of betrayal immediately gets healed as he gets to know about his wife's sufferings and misfortunes. Soon, he comes out of the room only to find Psyche lying in his mother's garden in an exhausted state. Instantly, he forgives her and then onwards, both start living happily in the magnificent palace. Psyche also convinces Eros to forgive his mother for all her cruel deeds that she had done to make Psyche suffer. Zeus gifts the drink of the Gods, Ambrosia, to Psyche to immortalise her. Surprisingly, after all this, Aphrodite also forgives Psyche as she starts residing in the sky with her husband, while the men on Earth, who have seemed to forget her for Psyche, again start worshipping her as the true Goddess of beauty.

The scholars of the Greek myth and religion have always found the figure of the Mother Goddesses to be fascinating as their narratives have helped to unravel various themes in the fields of psychology, anthropology, as well as women studies, thereby illuminating the role of the 'Great Mother' in the psychic and cultural life of humanity. C. G. Jung and his adherents have discovered a prolific sphere in the image of the 'Great Mother' for the implementation of their conjectures concerning the connection between ancient myth and human consciousness; their speculation regarding feminine psyche; and the role, women play in their family.

Both the ancient tales, i.e., the stories of Demeter and Persephone and Eros and Psyche, involve a central mother-figure along with a maiden, who is undergoing the journey of becoming a bride or a wife. Apart from that, in both the cases, a conflict emerges at the time of the marriage of the children, which will inevitably cause a breakage in the parent-child bond, thereby featuring great psychic turbulence for both the parent and the child. The two narratives, concerning the mother-daughter relationship and the mother-son bond, thus naturally yield insights into feminine psychology when examined through the lens of Jungian hypothesis, describing the emotional tensions involved in the rites of passage, commonly known by the name of 'marriage'; myth being a mirror of the human psyche.

Sigmund Freud, being the first in the twentieth century, to promote the notion that myth, similar to dream, facilitates an avenue towards exploring the human unconscious with its concealed wish-fulfilments, anxieties, and fantasies. Jung was his first follower to get fascinated by the recurrence of specific symbols in myths, dreams, art, as well as in literatures of diversified cultures and this instigated him to conceptualise the idea of 'collective unconsciousness'. According to the concept of Jung, this collective unconscious depicts the ancestral memory, which comprises various hereditary imageries, symbols, and themes, which aid in shaping human experiences, knowledge, and perceptions. These fragmented components of human memory contain four archetypes, which helps to constitute the human personality. They indicate the ambitions, values, morals, beliefs, and the motivations of human beings. The four archetypes as identified by Jung, the 'persona', the 'shadow', the 'anima' or 'animus' and the 'self' are thus outcomes of the collective and shared ancestral memories, which aren't visible to the naked eyes, but mostly feature in art, literature, and religion. These Jungian archetypes depict a journey of a man from his unconscious state to his individuation, thus merging the conscious and the unconscious part of the psyche.

The Jungian persona represents the various masks a person wears in different social context based on his culture, upbringing, and general environment as well as depending upon the company he is with or the people he is surrounded by, which helps him to adapt to his surroundings. In literature, the word 'persona' indicates the fictional characters, whose actions and behaviours make up the plot of the text. The Jungian philosophy asserts that every human being has a light side as well as a dark side within him. It is the light side which one willingly exhibits, thereby repressing the dark side. This dark side is called 'shadow' by Jung. This aspect of the human personality is neither appreciated nor given much attention to. It is known to reside in the unconscious state of the human mind and, very similar to the Freudian concept of 'unconscious mind', it consists of suppressed or subjugated memories and thoughts, which are to be realised in the guise of automatic responses. Prejudices and biases are features, which stem from the shadow that often tends to surface without giving a warning and often unintentionally. Since every man is a product of his upbringing and culture and the past experiences help to shape his perception of the world, he inevitably contains an ideal man or woman within him. The anima (woman) and the animus (man) is a demonstration of the opposite gender i.e., the ideal. The femininity in a man's psyche is represented by the anima, while the animus in a woman's psyche exhibits masculine features in her, but the society around deliberately subdues these opposing constructs. The ego often has the tendency of merging with the conscious and unconscious states of the psyche, thereby giving way to 'self'. This Jungian 'self' depicts the individuation in a man that is very similar to his individuality, which makes him unique and different from others. This particular 'self' helps to respect others' individuality; both their strengths and weaknesses.

Apart from these primary archetypes, Jung also talks about the other archetypes like the 'Old Man' and the 'Great Mother'. The archetype of the wise old man also known as 'Sensex', 'Sage' or 'Sophos', according to Carl Jung, is described as a classic figure in literature featuring a wise old man, distinguished for his wisdom and sound judgement. He often emerges as a God or Goddess, a magician or a wizard, a philosopher or an advisor, who play a significant role in the journey of the hero. The 'shadow' of the 'sage' cultivates the tendencies of having critical and dogmatic outlook in man. In the process of individuation, this archetype transpires late in human life as an indication of realisation of self –

> If an individual has wrestled seriously enough and long enough with the anima or animus problem… the unconscious again changes its dominant character and appears in a new symbolic form: as a masculine initiator and guardian (an Indian guru), a wise old man, a spirit of nature, and so forth. (Jung 207)

In the Jungian personality theory, the mother archetype plays a crucial role in the unconscious life of an individual, which constitutes the formative stages in the life of a child. Being the birth-giver, the sole sustainer, and nurturer in the infant's life for quite a long period of time, the mother tends to have an infinite amount of effect upon the child's conscious and unconscious development right from its birth. She has always been the chief source of life, nourishment, warmth, security, and all the essential and salubrious elements required for the child. Nevertheless, it has been observed that the same life giver and nurturer emerges to become a source of terror to the helpless child, who being totally dependent on her, often suffers from anxiety that the mother's care and nurture might be withdrawn at any point of time. This channel of goodness and love may transform occasionally into an event for anxiety and psychological discomfort for the child. These polarities observed in the mothers are called by the Jungian term – the 'Good Mother' and the 'Terrible Mother'. The 'Good Mother', having an all-caring, all-giving, beneficial, and generous attitude toward the child, can be found in different benevolent figures in folklore and myth; Demeter being a prime example of it. At the same time, the 'Terrible Mother' also appears in traditional tales of many cultures in the guise of a witch, wicked step-mother, or Gorgon. Both Persephone and Psyche feature in the ancient tales as an innocent, beautiful maiden or 'Kore' figure, ripe for marriage in the beginning, but ends being a damsel and bride. These feminine incarnations as examined by Jung have significant psychic implication, which is highlighted with great frequency in both myth and literature. W. I. Thompson summarises this context as –

> The three images of the goddess – maiden, matron, and old crone – present us with the three archetypal relationships of the female to the male: she is huge and calls us from the womb; she is beautiful and calls us to her bed; she is old and ugly and calls us to the tomb. (Thompson 142)

Jungian hermeneutics derives material for the assertion of the interplay of these three feminine archetypes from the stories of Persephone and Psyche. Homeric *Hymn to Demeter* begins with transporting the readers to the domain of women, where Persephone is found playing among other maidens in a tender world of girlish innocence. This serenity is brutally shattered by the harsh intrusion of Hades, who abducts the innocent Persephone violently against her will. Here, the poet informs the readers that Persephone in this crisis only thinks of her mother, her only secured shelter, and cries for help –

> While the goddess could still gaze at earth
> and starry heaven, strong rush of the fish abundant sea
> and sun's rays, she still hoped to see her dear mother

> and the race of gods who live forever:
> hope yet charmed her strong mind though she grieved.
> But the mountain peaks and the sea depths echoed
> with her eternal cry, and her goddess mother heard her. (Rayor 68)

Immediately, Demeter's heart aches –

> Sharp grief seized her heart; with both hands
> she tore the veil from her ambrosial hair,
> threw a black cloak across her shoulders
> and sped like a bird over the nourishing land and sea,
> searching: but none of the immortal gods
> or mortal folk would tell her the truth,
> nor did omen birds come bearing messages. (Rayor 68)

Jung and Kerenyi, in their collection *Essays on a Science of Mythology*, considers the figure of Demeter and Persephone as emblematic of two archetypal aspects of feminine consciousness –motherhood and maidenhood.

In the Homeric *Hymn to Demeter*, the intimacy between mother-daughter pair is depicted in such a manner as if Persephone, the daughter, belongs to her mother alone. Demeter or Δημήτηρ (Dēmḗtēr) gets her name from the ancient Greek words, γῆ (gê or 'earth') and μήτηρ (mḗtēr, or 'mother'), which incorporates her quintessential motherhood in it. Zeus as a father has a very little role in the life of a maiden; rather unsympathetically he has engineered her abduction to please his brother. Even when he has been appealed for help, he turns a deaf ear to her. Marilyn Arthur in an essay "Politics and Pomegranate: An Interpretation of the Homeric Hymn to Demeter" interpreted this dissolution of mother-maiden union at the hands of a male as "a statement of domination by the male, Olympian order over the female world." (Arthur 11) William H. Desmonde identifies this mother-daughter bond with the defloration ceremonies of primitive female puberty rites. Bruce Lincoln on the other hand deciphers the rape of Persephone in terms of initiation into mature womanhood. Jung similarly views the separation of Demeter and Persephone as the process of individuation. He states that an infant is born undifferentiated from its mother and develops an identity closely fused to her, but the natural course of events will aid to develop an independent and a unique personality in it and in turn the child tends to lose ties with the mother in order to form his or her own identity. The various rites of passage involved with this process can be comprehended as different types of death. Marriage being the central rite of passage in a maiden's life holds repercussions not only for the maiden herself, but also for her mother, since her union with her husband will definitely necessitate distancing if not separation between a mother and daughter. This intrusion of the husband in the mother-daughter bond will trigger multiple emotions like grief, fear, and rage. In Demeter's case, these unpleasant emotions, as pointed out by Froma Zeitlin in "Cultic Models of the Female: Rites of Dionysus and Demeter", which has got initiated due to her daughter's forceful admission into the mysteries of sexuality, affects directly the fertility of the land. Homer through the *Hymn* tries to unravel this painful and darker aspect of marriage.

The next element that draws our attention to the criticism and analysis of the *Homeric Hymn* is the husband of Persephone being the God of Death and the marriage being initiated through severity against her wish, which Neumann undermines to consider it to be a possibility of being an accidental imagination in the plot. He rather determines the motif of the marriage of death in the narrative, which is one of the central archetypes of the feminine mysteries, where either the maiden dies on the wedding day or she encounters with death. According to Neumann, there can be another variation of the tale which depicts the maiden to transpire into a sacrificial victim at the hands of some monster or beast instead of becoming a bride as in case of Eurydice, Oedipus's wife, who dies on the day of her wedding; Alcestis' destiny is decided on her marriage day; Iphigenia, lured to death by her own father, who had promise to get her married; and Antigone, whom Sophocles' pen has given in marriage to death. However, the Jungian school had asserted that the motif of 'Marriage of Death' features in the feminine psyche rather than in the historical chronicles as girls inevitably have to pass through a traumatic stage during her journey from maidenhood to wifehood.

> It becomes particularly clear how decisive the transition from maiden-flower to fruit-mother must be in the life of the feminine, when we consider how quickly women age under primitive conditions, how quickly the strength of the fertile mother is consumed by hard work. The transition from girlhood to womanhood is always felt more keenly where, as so frequently happens, a carefree youth is immediately followed by the constraint and regularity of adulthood and marriage. (Neumann 64)

The period which marks marriage as a rite of passage, resulting in the death of maidenhood as well as the birth of wifehood, is often considered to serve as a metaphor to death itself, which marks the transition from the earthly life to the life after death. Similarly, Persephone's transformation from being a carefree maiden into the Queen of the underworld (Death) shares the same shattering image. Although Hades never appears to be a torturous husband, yet he can never replace Demeter's place in the life of Persephone. She regains her joy only when Hermes facilitates her reunion with her mother. At the same time, it is a fact that she can never restore her old self. Hades tricks her into eating the seeds of the pomegranate; a symbolic representation of tasting sexuality, which will never again allow her to revert back to her naive and virgin self, being only the daughter of her mother. She has to divide herself between her husband and mother, and hence she must spend two-third part of the year with Demeter and the other one-third part with Hades. In Jungian terms, thus the Homeric *Hymn to Demeter* projects the sorrow, loss, and resentment involved in the shadow side of marriage and individuation.

The same tension of the Demeter-Persephone myth is also observed to be shared by the narrative of Eros and Psyche, where a central mother figure resisting the marriage of her child is featured. In this case, it is a son in place of a daughter, who is the victim of the mother's unconstrained obsession. The characters of this narrative similarly suffer the same anxiety, grief, and resentment like the earlier one. The tale begins with the description of Psyche, who is young, beautiful, nubile, and is on the threshold of a rite of passage as in case of Persephone. In this instance too, Psyche's marriage to Eros will be a marriage of death, though unlike Persephone's husband, Hades, the God of the Underworld (death), her husband, is the God of love. The Oracle of Delphi, right at the beginning, has predicted and explained Psyche's wedding in terms of a funeral.

> 'Let Psyche's corpse be clad in mourning weed
> and set on rock of yonder hill aloft:
> Her husband is no wight of human seed.
> But serpent dire and fierce as may be thought.
> Who flies with wings above in starry skies
> And doth subdue each thing with fiery flight.
> The gods themselves and powers that seem so wise
> With mighty Jove be subject to his might;
> The rivers black and deadly floods of pain
> And darkness eke as thrall to him remain.' (Adlington 194)

The rite that accomplishes the command of the oracle can be interpreted as a vivid elucidation of the imagery of the marriage of death. Apuleius describes –

> But necessity compelled that poor Psyche should be brought to her appointed doom, according to the divine commandment; and when the solemnity of the wretched wedding was ended with great sorrow, all the people followed the living corpse, and they went to bring this sorrowful spouse, not to her. (Adlington 196)

The narrative unfolds the irony of the situation when it recounts the involvement of the funeral wedding torches, ululation replacing the hymeneal, and the bridal veil being used to wipe away tears.

Besides, the element of the 'Marriage of Death', another common archetype links the two narratives, i.e., abduction. Both Psyche and Persephone have been abducted to get married. Their first encounter with male sexuality has never been peaceful or happy. They are held hostage by their male partners without being asked or rather without their consent. The pre-nuptial anxieties have gained concrete expression in case of Psyche when she wonders whether her lover is a snaky monster or not, and for Persephone, her husband being literally the king of the realm of darkness. The apprehension of Psyche has always been interpreted by Jacques Barchilón in terms of human psychology as –

> The very existence of the monster in the Psyche myth and in the fairy tale has a meaning. There must be a reason for the human mind to associate sex with bestiality. The idea of falling in love has dangerous connotations; it is tainted with the taboos and prohibitions from childhood. For the child consciously thinks that sex is terrible. And as he grows, he cannot quite readily reconcile himself to the simple truth that sex is not terrifying. This belief is prohibited by conventions which cannot allow that sex is "normal." Thus it is no wonder that in fantasies, dreams, and fairy tales sex is presented as dangerous and readily symbolized as "the monster." (Barchilón 20)

Thus, both the narratives relate the story of the death of maidenhood, which is accompanied by the fear of a mysterious male figure, whom the maiden encounters unwillingly. Nevertheless, both the marriages considerably vary from each other in their final outcomes. The marriage of Persephone and Hades continues to remain frozen and barren, but after a series of events, Eros and Psyche's union undergoes a profound transformation. When Eros deserts Psyche and returns to his mother, Psyche has been able to successfully and willingly recover from her anxieties and emerge to be a dedicated wife, who can go to any extent to bring back her lost husband. She readily endures all the tortures for him. She addresses her invisible partner, conveying that –

> My honey, my husband, I had rather die an hundred times than be separate from your sweet company; for whosoever you be, I love and retain you within my heart, as if you were mine own spirit, and I make you not less than if you were Cupid himself ... (Adlington 209)

This proves to be an astounding reversal of the relationship between Persephone and Hades. She has passed through three difficult tests to fulfil her act of 'catabasis' and thus turns out to be triumphant in bringing the rite of passage to a happy ending, thereby securing both the love of Eros as well as his mother's blessings. The 'Marriage of Death' finally ends with a celebration of life for her though it involved several vicissitudes and trials.

Aphrodite very similar to Demeter suffers from an apprehension of losing her child in marriage, but otherwise they both significantly vary from each other. Much unlike Demeter, she is jealous, enraged, cruel, and manipulative throughout the narrative and thus represents the Jungian concept of the 'Terrible Mother' and is often considered to be parallel to the concept of Walsh – "the folk-tale queen whose hitherto peerless beauty is excelled by that of a simple maiden." (Walsh 200) Her son has always been overly possessive towards her and thus she takes this advantage, attempting to dispose her rival from the very beginning through him. Her rage and envy reach the extreme point when she discovers that her 'paelex' has emerged to be her son's love object. Here also, one can notice a hint of the Oedipal Complex especially when she manipulates her maternal love to manoeuvre Eros in agreeing to afflict Psyche with incestuous eroticism. She kisses her son to get her work done, who himself has been then in the process of individuation, fearing to lose control over her son. She also vents her anger upon the maiden by plaguing her with her pettiness and jealousy. Bruno Bettelheim describes this situation in "Freud and soul" –

> A mother's love for her son and her jealous rage against the girl he prefers to her can be openly acknowledged. That the young girl surpasses the mature woman in beauty, that a son turns away from his mother to embrace his bride, that a bride has to suffer from the jealousy of her lover's mother – all this, although extremely troublesome, accords with normal human emotions, and is in line with the natural conflict of the generations. (Bettelheim 60)

Aphrodite thus finally attempts accommodating with the child's spouse as in the case of Demeter in order to avoid their parent-child relationship from getting threatened. Though Demeter can never overcome her antipathy towards her son-in-law, but Aphrodite ultimately at the end of the narrative accepts the inevitable. The 'Terrible mother' has at last changed herself into a 'Good Mother'. The tale also recounts the journey of Eros, who starts off his life being irresponsible, immature, and a subject to maternal whim –

> Then by and by she called her winged son Cupid, rash enough and hardy, who by his evil manners, contemning all public justice and law, armed with (ire and arrows, running up and down in the nights from house to house, and corrupting the lawful marriages of every person, doth nothing (and yet he is not punished) but that which is evil ... (Adlington 191)

He finally gains maturity and ends up being a loving and responsible husband, but at the cost of his individuation from his mother, passing through the rite of passage. At the same time, he also ends his journey being at peace with his mother. It is very important to highlight a significant difference between the two tales – Apuleius's *Cupid and Psyche* and the Greek myth, Homer's *Hymn to Demeter*. The Greek myth ends with the reunion of the mother and the daughter, but it dwells on the shadow side of marriage, while Apuleius's tale although depicts many dark elements, but it presents a psychologically satisfying narrative by transforming the 'Marriage of Death' to marriage being the source of life. The mothers and the maidens in the story give Carl Jung his archetypes, which become universal symbols, enlightening various human experiences in the real world.

Works Cited

Adlington, W. Trans. *Apuleius the Golden Ass being the Metamorphoses of Lucius Apuleius.* W. William Heinemann ltd. and G. P. Putnam's sons, 1915.

Apuleius. qtd. in Anon. "Eros and Psyche," https://www.greeka.com/greece-myths/eros-psyche/. Accessed 12 Jul. 2022.

Arthur, Marylin. "Politics and Pomegranates: an Interpretation of the Homeric Hymn to Demeter". The Homeric Hymn to Demeter: Translation, Commentary, and Interpretive Essays. Edited by Helene P. Foley, Princeton University Press, 2013. https://doi.org/10.1515/9781400849086-024. Accessed 25 May. 2022.

Barchilón, Jacques. "Beauty and the Beast: From Myth to Fairy Tale." *Psychoanalysis and the Psychoanalytic Review,* 46 (1959).

Eliade, Mircea. qtd. in Anon. "Chapter VIII: Lust or Strength Demeter/ Persephone," https://zero-point.tripod.com/pantheon/Demeter.html. Accessed 24 May. 2022.

Jung, C. G. a. "The Psychological Aspects of the Kore". *Collected Works of C.G. Jung Vol.9 Part 1*. Edited by Gerhard Adler and R. F.C. Hull, https://doi.org/10.1515/9781400850969.182. Accessed 24 May. 2022.

———. b. *Man and His Symbols.* Bantam Doubleday Dell Publishing Group Inc, 1964.

Lawson, Christine Ann. Understanding the Borderline Mother: Helping Her Children Transcend the Intense, Unpredictable, and Volatile Relationship. Rowman & Littlefield, 2002.

Luke, Helen. "The Mother- Daughter Mysteries." *Woman: Earth and Spirit.* Crossroad, 1982.

Morford, Mark P. O. And Robert J. Lenardon. *Classical Mythology.* Oxford University Press, 1999.

Neumann, Erich. *Amor and Psyche: The Psychic Development of the Feminine. A Commentary on the Tale by Apuleius*. Translated by Ralph Manheim. Princeton Univ. Press, 1971.

Rayor, Diane J. *Homeric Hymn to Demeter*. Grand Valley State University, 1998.

Roth, Kimberlee, and Freda B. Friedman. *Surviving a Borderline Parent: How to Heal Your Childhood Wounds & Build Trust, Boundaries, and Self-esteem.* New Harbinger Publications, 2003.

Thompson, William Irwin. *The Time Falling Bodies Take to Light.* St. Martin's, 1981.

Walsh, P.G. *The Roman Novel*. Cambridge Univ. Press, 1970.

IV

The Legacy of Love: Exploring Father–Son Relationships

There had been a custom in the Greek society in ancient times which was recognised by law as well as by society that every individual was obligated to take care of their parents in their old age, which was known by the term '*Gêrotrophia*'; the very concept emerging from the notion of *anchisteia* (kinship). Solon, an Athenian statesman, lawmaker, and poet, who has been famous for his efforts to fight against all political, economic, and moral decline in archaic Athens, had designed a law to compel the Athenians to perform their duty of paying for the *trephein* (nurture) of their fathers and mothers as well as their forefathers or ancestors, who are still alive. This particular law was mentioned within the sixth degree of kingship, detailing the limits of *anchisteia*.

In the Roman society, the authoritative control of the fathers was over their kin till they were alive, i.e., till the *paterfamilias* (the head of the family) lived; the age of the sons never mattered. After the death of the head of the family, the power would get transferred to the immediate descendant, who was acquitted from *patria potestas* (power or control of the father), since he became the next *paterfamilias*, thereby gaining authority over the other descendants as well as the entire family property. Thus, a son of the family, known by the word '*filiusfamilias*', irrespective of his age, could never own any property until he became a *paterfamilias* himself. Before that, he could only have control over the *peculium* (a particular sum of money given to him by his father), which he could claim to be his own, though the amount legally belonged to his father, who could at any point of time withdraw it according to his wish. Even a son could never count on his father's inheritance as being the *paterfamilias,* he possessed the right to disinherit his children as per his will without giving any explanation.

Ancient scholars like Paul Veyne and Yan Thomas had indicated that the existing law of the time had made the relationship between fathers and children difficult, complicated, and problematic. Frequent cases of patricide were recorded which troubled the Roman political authorities and the entire legal system. To reduce such instances, Roman Emperor

Vespasian in the first century CE (69-79 CE) introduced a law that a creditor could never claim money lent to a man (*paterfamilias*) from his son (*filiusfamilias*) after his death. This decree of the *senatus consultum* (ancient Roman senate) was called '*Macedonianum*'.

Similarly, a father was not obligated to pay a debt contracted by his son, which appeared to be both convenient as well as inconvenient for the *paterfamilias*. In the second century BCE, the praetor (Roman magistrate) intervened through the introduction of a new law named *actiones adiecticiae qualitatis*, which allowed the creditors of a son to get back the money they owed from the *paterfamilias* (his father). A son was only successful in his economic ventures if his father could afford to pay his debts. The son's creditor could exact his money from the father in its entirety only under two circumstances – one, if the father had nominated his son to be the head of a business or secondly, if the father had particularly authorised his creditor as well as his son to conclude together the arrangement that had initiated the debt. In case of any failure of the deal, in the first case, the creditor could charge the *paterfamilias* with the *actio exercitoria* or the *actio institoria*, and in the second case, with *actio quod iussu*. Apart from this, fathers were only accountable for the *peculium* (the property held by a person by virtue of being a wife, child, or slave) given to the sons, or for the benefits that they personally received from their son's activity (*actio de peculio et de in rem verso*).

Augustus introduced a new *peculium*, which granted a bit more freedom to adult sons as compared to earlier times. A son had been permitted to acquire some money by rendering military service to the state and along with that he could make over the property of this *peculium* in his will. Hadrian next went one step further and gave the sons the right to dispose of it *inter vivos* (made or given among living people). However, the son who still remained in the patria potestas was compelled to assume the role of the *paterfamilias* as far as the military *peculium* was concerned. As a result, a father had the power of suing his son from the obligations related to the *peculium castrense* (benefits or money acquired in military service), but the reverse could not be done, i.e., a son did not have the right to sue his father. The position of the sons and the slaves in the family was not very different except that when the *paterfamilias* passed away, the slaves could continue with their job, belonging to a new *dominus*, though they had a choice of *manumission* (release from slavery); whereas the sons and the daughters had a chance of emancipation by becoming the *sui iuris* (of one's own right), i.e., they could acquire the legal independence but only in the field of private law. Lastly, it has been found that in those days the economic disability of a *filiusfamilias* often led to his enslavement. The power once enjoyed by a *paterfamilias* to sell his son into slavery (*ius vendendi*) had been mitigated by law. The Twelve Tables however states that if a son is sold thrice by his father, he gets free from paternal power (*si pater filium ter venum duit filius a patre liber esto*). The Republic censors had always utilised the *nota censoria* in such case to introduce such fathers to public blame and never allowed them to enter the senate. Moreover, there were certain situations, where it was socially permissible to a father to sell his son into slavery – in case of a *delictum* (an illicit act), committed by a son and punishable by a private *actio poenalis* like *furtum* (theft), *rapina* (a violent theft) and *damnum iniuria* (outrage or damage to another property), which ended with a pecuniary contamination. There were other difficulties in the social lives of the children which often ruined their personal lives. In fact, a son or a daughter did not have the right to choose his or her marriage partner against the father's consent. The jurist Paulus noted, "Marriage does not exist unless everyone consents, that is those who come together and those under whose power they are" (Nussbaum and Sihvola 273), while another source found, "A marriage is valid if ... both parties consent, if they are independent (*sui iuris*), or their parents too, if they are in power" (Cantarella 290), which confirms that a father alone had the power to control the private lives of the children. He could make as well as break his child's marriage, disregarding his or her will. However, in the second century C.E., emperor Antonius Pius abolished the paternal right and thus prohibited fathers from interfering in their children's lives.

The law of *Patria Potestas* was a matter of pride for the Romans, but there was no such technical term or phrase corresponding to it in the Greek culture, which indicates that perhaps in ancient Greece there was no institution having similar characteristics. Hans Julius Wolff marked the difference between the Greek and the Roman families, stating that although they were recognised as manifestations of the same patriarchal structure, the *oikos* (the family, the family property, or the house) of the Greeks was considered to be a collective unity comprising of multiple persons, things, and rituals, which was unlike the Roman *familia* (family), being more individualistic and strongly centred on the single person of the paterfamilias.

Unlike the Roman laws, Athens had a totally different custom and law regarding the inheritance. Primarily, the father's dominance or authority over the sons was not perennial; rather it existed till the children attained a certain age. The Athenian laws were less stringent than the

Roman laws. The *ius vitae ac necis* (right to live or source of life) of the Roman law was absent in the Athenian legal system. At the most, a father could exert *apokeryxis* (break the tie with the son) on his son, by which he could disinherit him from the *oikos*. Demosthenes, a Greek statesman and ancient Athenian orator, recounted that as a father had the right to name his son, similarly a law had been introduced by which he could *apokeryxai* (disinherit) them, but he did not specify the grounds on which he could do so. Unfortunately, there were no other sources in which the concept was mentioned.

Aristotle further highlighted another side of the parent-child law, explaining that a father might anytime disown and disinherit his son from the family or the family property, but a son could not disown his father. He explained the reason behind this inequality evident in the law by drawing a comparison between debtors and sons. A debtor, he asserted, was bound to repay his debt, but on the other hand, a son would never give back that he had inherited from his father. This justifies appropriately that as a creditor could willingly remit the debit, a father could also disown his sons, but there was a condition attached to it. A father could only disinherit his son if he exceeded in perversity. Instances are found in several anecdotes that fathers or tutors had discussed the possibility of disowning their sons or pupils, but fearing the consequences, they often ignored their son's perverseness as they wanted to avoid getting penalised for their deeds. There is scarce evidence of the fact that the law on *apokeryxai* used to turn the ethic principle of the filial hierarchical subordination of fathers in case of a legal rule, though the value of it was ideological or hypothetical instead of being real, since no such cases are found to have been recorded in any document. Apart from this, Aristotle had identified a confusion regarding the matter; it is difficult to determine the extremity of the perverseness in case of a son, which demanded the application of the law. There was no parameter of judgement. One can only envisage the situation that enabled the family name to be disgraced and dishonoured due to the son, which could only be mended by disowning him. Hence, it can be inferred that the theoretical presence of *apokeryxai* could not affect the mildness of the Athenian paternal power. Nevertheless, Solon decided to formulate the law of gêrotrophia.

Solon, being a reputed Athenian lawmaker, resolved to take resort to the legal system to thrust upon the children the moral and social duty to take responsibility of their parents in their old age. *Gêrotrophia* mainly aimed at putting a limit to the case of abandonment of elderly parents. Surprisingly, it has been found that certain categories of people were exempted from this moral and social law as identified by Aeschines, Plutarch, and others, which include the children who were forced into prostitution by their own father and their prime role was to provide burial; children, who were born by *hetairai* (courtesan); and children, who were never taught any *techne*, that includes mainly crafts, though agriculture could not be ignored. Anyone else violating the law of Solon would be prosecuted with a lawsuit named *graphe goneon kakoseos*, which caused the convict to lose both political and civil rights. Lysias, an ancient orator, had recounted that another lawsuit called *nomos kakoseos* inflicted death penalty on the accused for beating his parents, for denying them assistance in their old age, or if an adopted son was found to sneak his father's property. It can be deduced from a document of the late 4th or 3rd century BCE that *gêrotrophia* was not only proposed but also approved in Delphi, and ordered to recopy following a previous record, which proves that it was established even before this occasion, but the exact record of the manner of punishment is not found yet. In Athens, the prisons were used to keep the accused in custody, while they would be waiting for their final verdict. This Delphic penalty was probably a monetary compensation rather an *atimia* (disenfranchisement). The accused was kept in custody for obtaining the payment of the penalty. In Athens, *graphe goneon kakoseos* ensured the rights of the patrimony, thereby guaranteeing the elder members of the family their right of *gêrotrophia*.

In this context, another term is quite relevant and demands mention – *threpteria* (*threptra* or *tropheia*). It can be defined as the 'cost of nurture', which was to be paid through embracing death while protecting the father, and thus it has been considered to be quite pathetic. The term was first introduced in the work of Homer as the formula for the young men's death, though the concept appeared in both Homer and Hesiod's works.

James Redfield, in his critical work, *Nature and Culture in the Iliad*, asserted that the relationship between fathers and sons in the Homeric society was considered to be fundamental. Homer's *Iliad* is undoubtedly an epic poem recounting the brawl between two great warriors near the end of the Trojan War, but it cannot be denied that the narrative sustains a coherent perspective of parental dedication and devotion as well as a centrality of the parent-child bond. Louise Pratt in his article, "The Parental Ethos of the Iliad", rightly commented that – "the overall ethos of the Iliad is a parental one, that is, one characterized by personal sacrifice and significant investment in the care and protection of loved ones". (Pratt 25)

Homer recounted some of the significant events of the tenth year of the Trojan War; a tension breaks among the Achaeans when the Greek army successfully sacks Chryse, an allied town of Troy. The war spurred due to the abduction of Helen, the wife of king of Sparta, Menelaus, but in the course of the battle, the Achaeans has captivated two beautiful maidens, Chryseis and Briseis, whom the leader of the Achaean forces, Agamemnon, and the greatest warrior of Greece, Achilles, take as their prize respectively. Meanwhile, Chryses, the father of Chryseis, who used to serve as a priest in the temple of Apollo, presents a huge ransom in exchange for his daughter, but Agamemnon does not agree to return her. Enraged with this disobedience, Apollo sends a plague upon the Achaean camp, which causes the death of many Achaean armies. Perplexed Agamemnon, unable to find any reason and solution, takes resort to the prophet Calchas, from whom he gets to know that Chryseis is the real cause. There remains no other way except to give Chryseis up, but he immediately demands Briseis from Achilles in her place. Achilles considers it to be an insult and instantly returns to his tent in the camp. He makes up his mind not to fight for the Achaean any longer and vengefully pleads with his mother Thetis, a sea-nymph, to urge the King of Gods Zeus to destroy the entire Greek force. At that moment, both the sides have declared a cease fire with one another and this time Zeus heeds to the Trojans' entreaty for help and support.

The situation seems to be highly unfavourable for the Achaeans as Zeus starts aiding the Trojans, while Achilles declines to fight for them. This continues for quite a number of days. Several fierce duels have been fought between Paris and Menelaus and between Hector and Ajax. The Achaean suffers great loss and makes no progress. The Trojans start to push back the Achaean army. Even the efforts of the Achaeans warrior Diomedes, who is considered next to Achilles in heroism, cannot save the Greeks. Diomedes and Odysseus bring some information regarding the secret scheme of the Trojans, which brings some hope to the Achaeans, but the next day seems all the more disastrous. The Trojans break through the Greek embankments, advancing towards the boundaries of their camp and setting one of their ships on fire. Day by day, it gets more prominent that defeat is inevitable without the ships as the armies cannot return or escape and have to stay back only to get destroyed. This situation troubles Achilles, but he is still reluctant to help the Greeks fight with the Trojan army as it may enable him to compromise with his honour. Achilles decides to agree to Nestor's plan and gives permission to Patroclus, his most beloved friend, to take his place in the war by wearing his special armour, given to him by his mother. Ultimately, with the help of Patroclus, the Achaeans successfully push the Trojan Army from the ships and back to the city walls. Just then, Apollo knocks Patroclus' armour and Hector gets a chance to slay him immediately. The Achaeans are able to bring back the body of Patroclus after much struggle and confusion, though they had to lose the divine armour to the Trojans. The tragic sight of Patroclus's corpse brings a change in Achilles and he instantly decides to avenge his friend's death. He initiates reconciliation with Agamemnon and the Greeks and appeals to Thetis to get him a new set of armour from Hephaestus. With this, he sets off to lead the Achaean army once again.

Hector meanwhile is much relieved since Achilles is not participating in the war and hence he allows his men to camp outside the wall of the city. Just then, the sight of Achilles totally shocks them and as they attempt to flee behind the city wall, they get slain by Achilles. Achilles also fights with Xanthus, the God of River, who gets furious seeing the number of corpses that are falling into its streams due to Achilles. At last, he ultimately calls Hector for a duel outside the wall of Troy, which Hector accepts instead of joining his comrades in their escape to the city, being ashamed of the inappropriate order he has given to his force. Three times Hector makes Achilles chase him around the periphery of the city, but finally Goddess Athena tricks Hector into confronting Achilles. A fearful fight breaks out and Hector gets slaughtered by Achilles. He then fastens his dead body to the back of the chariot and drags him to the Achaean camp, where a grand funeral is arranged for Patroclus, which includes various athletic games in his honour. For the next nine days, Achilles drags his corpse in a circular manner around the funeral pyre of Patroclus. Finally, the epic poem ends with the Gods deciding that Hector must get a proper burial and hence Zeus sends Hermes to escort his father King Priam to the Achaean camp, where he begs his son's dead body with tears, which melts Achilles's heart. He decides to give Hector's corpse to the Trojans so that he receives the hero's funeral.

In the whole text of *Iliad*, the father-son dynamic acts as a dominant theme, elucidating how their relationships are not just biological, but also emotional. They have immense pride and respect for one another. The sons are expected to follow their fathers' footsteps to become noble warriors and also protect their fathers' name and honour, and in doing so, often they are seen to put their lives at risk. There are many such examples of father-son pairs in this epic poem, which attract the readers' attention. Among them, the first and most tragic relationship is between Priam and Hector.

Priam in *Iliad* is known to be the last king of Troy, who has succeeded King Laomedon and has extended his kingdom beyond the Hellespont. His first wife is the daughter of Merops the seer, Arisbe, and next he marries Hecuba and then many others. Homer relates that he has fifty sons and many daughters; among them nineteen are bore by Hecuba, which include Priam's two most favourite sons, Hector and Paris. During the Trojan War, he has been old and powerless. He has to see his thirteen sons die with his own eyes. The great Achaean warrior Achilles in a single day killed his three sons – Polydorus, Lycaon, and Hector.

Priam's profound love and concern for his favourite son Hector is revealed in *Book 22.* Hector's parents make sincere effort to prevent him from facing Achilles, while he was waiting for him outside the Scaean Gates.

"Have mercy on me, O my son! revere
The words of age; attend a parent's prayer!
If ever thee in these fond arms I press'd,
Or still'd thy infant clamours at this breast;
Ah do not thus our helpless years forego,
But, by our walls secured, repel the foe.
Against his rage if singly thou proceed,
Should'st thou, (but Heaven avert it!) should'st thou bleed,
Nor must thy corse lie honour'd on the bier,
Nor spouse, nor mother, grace thee with a tear!
Far from our pious rites those dear remains
Must feast the vultures on the naked plains." (Homer a 645)

Priam especially tries various means to deter his son from fighting with his enemy, i.e., by uttering a groan, beating his head with his hands, raising his hands up, and stretching his arms out. He begs his son to listen to him.

"Ah stay not, stay not! Guardless and alone;
Hector! My loved, my dearest, bravest son!
Methinks already I behold thee slain,
And stretch'd beneath that fury of the plain.
Implacable Achilles! Might'st thou be
To all the gods no dearer than to me!
Thee, vultures wild should scatter round the shore.
And bloody dogs grow fiercer from thy gore.
How many valiant sons I late enjoy'd,
Valiant in vain! By thy cursed arm destroy'd:
Or, worse than slaughtered, sold in distant isles

To shameful bondage, and unworthy toils.
Two, while I speak, my eyes in vain explore,
Two from one mother sprung, my Polydore,
And loved Lycaon; now perhaps no more!
Oh! If in yonder hostile camp they live,
What heaps of gold, what treasures would I give!
(Their grandsire's wealth, by right of birth their own,
Consign'd his daughter with Lelegia's throne:)
But if (which Heaven forbid) already lost,
All pale they wander on the Stygian coast;
What sorrows then must their sad mother know,
What anguish I? unutterable woe!
Yet less that anguish, less to her, to me,
Less to all Troy, if not deprived of thee.
Yet shun Achilles! Enter yet the wall;
And spare thyself, thy father, spare us all!
Save thy dear life; or, if a soul so brave
Neglect that thought, thy dearer glory save.
Pity, while yet I live, these silver hairs;
While yet thy father feels the woes he bears,
Yet cursed with sense! A wretch, whom in his rage\
(All trembling on the verge of helpless age)
Great Jove has placed, sad spectacle of pain!
The bitter dregs of fortune's cup to drain:
To fill with scenes of death his closing eyes,
And number all his days by miseries!
My heroes slain, my bridal bed o'erturn'd,
My daughters ravish'd, and my city burn'd,
My bleeding infants dash'd against the floor;
These I have yet to see, perhaps yet more!
Perhaps even I, reserved by angry fate,
The last sad relic of my ruin'd state,
(Dire pomp of sovereign wretchedness!) must fall,
And stain the pavement of my regal hall;
Where famish'd dogs, late guardians of my door,
Shall lick their mangled master's spatter'd gore.
Yet for my sons I thank ye, gods! 'tis well;
Well have they perish'd, for in fight they fell.
Who dies in youth and vigour, dies the best,
Struck through with wounds, all honest on the breast.

But when the fates, in fulness of their rage,
Spurn the hoar head of unresisting age,
In dust the reverend lineaments deform,
And pour to dogs the life-blood scarcely warm:
This, this is misery! The last, the worse,
That man can feel! Man, fated to be cursed!" (Homer a 643)

This long speech of Priam brings out the confusion within him. He is torn between two opposing forces – father versus king and parental desire versus heroic dictates. Nevertheless, it has been evident that his paternal role often seems to outweigh his royal one since his words express every emotion from the perspective of a father rather than that of a Trojan king. His hard feelings towards Achilles are not because he belongs to the enemy side, but he blames him for robbing him of most of his sons. He breaks down not because his land and people have been ruined by the Achaean army, but because his family has been disintegrated in the war. In the war between Hector and Achilles, there may be two possible outcomes – if Hector wins, the city Troy can be saved along with the family honour, but if he is defeated and slew, his family will be decomposed. Priam cannot help himself from thinking from a paternal point of view; the latter worries him all the more. He could not help but attempts to abstain his son from participating in the war. He subordinates his royal identity, instead only considers his son's survival along with his people's salvation to be his only concern, and thus in doing so his paternal persona overshadows his royal persona. He begs his son to fulfil his three wishes – firstly, to save himself from Achilles, who is far mightier; secondly, he wants him to stay inside the city walls so that the Greeks do not get a chance to kill the Trojans and enjoy glory; and lastly, he urges him to stay alive in order to protect him in his old age. Unfortunately, none of his goading gets fulfilled as the duel cannot save the killing of Priam's son, the enslavement of his daughters and daughter-in-laws, the death of the king, the ripping of naked corpses, and the drinking of blood by dogs.

The theme of paternal desire versus heroic dictates explored in Priam's appeal to Hector to avoid fighting with Achilles appears to be clearly at odds with the values of the royal society. In doing so, he fails to realise that he is actually instigating his son to defy the heroic code, which he has himself once imparted into his sons. According to K. Crotty, his pleading to the emotion of *eleos* (compassion and pity) – "the pathos inherent in the relation between the aged father and his son is perhaps nowhere clearer than in Priam's anguished plea to Hector to return to the safety of Troy, and not to face certain death at Achilles' hands'. (Crotty 36) However, if Hector has to pay heed to *eleos* and consider his parent's plea, then he will have violated the heroic values of *aidos* (the feeling of reverence, shame, and modesty) since "the emotions of aidos and eleos are in tension: Each flows from and supports values that do not easily coexist with each other" (Crotty 37). Apart from this, Hector also considers it important to battle with Achilles since by doing so, he will not only be able to abide by the heroic code of conduct, but also he will be able to save his father's dignity. Priam's plea evinces the fact that "the heroic values of prestige and fame … have their ultimate basis in the ardour of the ties binding father and son" (Crotty 37).

Interdependence and reciprocity constitute the basis of the relationship between Priam and Hector. Though it becomes quite obvious and expected that Priam has to suffer the loss of Hector, the moment he decides to war, but his way of lamentation is absolutely a rarity. He wails pitifully, tosses himself in the mud, and hastily decides to intrude on the Achaean camp to bring back his son's corpse. His royal persona seems to vanish as he overtly speaks before his people as an unfortunate father, who has lost his whole world –

"What make ye here, officious crowds! (he cries).
Hence! Nor obtrude your anguish on my eyes.
Have ye no griefs at home, to fix ye there:
Am I the only object of despair?
Am I become my people's common show,
Set up by Jove your spectacle of woe?
No, you must feel him too; yourselves must fall;
The same stern god to ruin gives you all:
Nor is great Hector lost by me alone;
Your sole defence, your guardian power is gone!
I see your blood the fields of Phrygia drown,
I see the ruins of your smoking town!
O send me, gods! Ere that sad day shall come,
A willing ghost to Pluto's dreary dome!" (Homer a 718)

He himself confides further that the death of his other sons has not grieved him so much as it is in case of Hector, which clearly shows that he is his favourite son. He feels as if this grief will take him directly to the House of Hades; he wishes to undergo a virtual death. He can neither enjoy food nor sleep. His final wish is to hold his son in his arms to mourn his death, which portrays him as a tragic father-figure. He even implores his remaining nine sons that he can bear the death of all, if Hector is there with him. He declares that he is ready to die once he clasps Hector's body and finally grieves for him. In *Book 24*, where Priam reaches Achilles' tent with Hermes to beg his son's dead body, the readers get further insight into his love for his son.

> "Inglorious sons of an unhappy sire!
> Why did not all in Hector's cause expire?
> Wretch that I am! My bravest offspring slain.
> You, the disgrace of Priam's house, remain!
> Mestor the brave, renown'd in ranks of war,
> With Troilus, dreadful on his rushing car,
> And last great Hector, more than man divine,
> For sure he seem'd not of terrestrial line!
> All those relentless Mars untimely slew,
> And left me these, a soft and servile crew,
> Whose days the feast and wanton dance employ,
> Gluttons and flatterers, the contempt of Troy!
> Why teach ye not my rapid wheels to run,
> And speed my journey to redeem my son?" (Homer a 719)

Instead of mourning the loss of the warrior and protector of the Trojans, he bewails the loss of his son. He knows that if he visits the Achaean camp, his own life as well as his whole nation will be at risk, but he does not care about anything. He decides to confront with the enemy side not as a king but as a bereaved old father. This journey can be considered as an informal journey, traditionally pertaining to katabatic narratives. He believes in the universal father-son bond and hence feels confident that he can sway his son's assassinator, Achilles' intransigence.

> "O first and greatest! Heaven's imperial lord!
> On lofty Ida's holy hill adored!
> To stern Achilles now direct my ways,
> And teach him mercy when a father prays.
> If such thy will, despatch from yonder sky
> Thy sacred bird, celestial augury!
> Let the strong sovereign of the plumy race
> Tower on the right of yon ethereal space;
> So shall thy suppliant, strengthen'd from above,
> Fearless pursue the journey mark'd by Jove." (Homer a 721)

Here again, the readers can encounter Priam's fatherly persona in place of his identity as a king. He disregards the risk involved in the action and gives no attention to Hecuba's appeal to stop him from going to the enemy's den. She warns him of the ruthlessness of Achilles and tells him that he will surely kill him, but he remains firm in his decision.

Apollo sends Iris to Priam in disguise to coerce him as he feels that Hector deserves a proper funeral, but when she reaches Troy, she finds him in the treasure chamber, accumulating valuables to offer Achilles as a ransom to get back his son's corpse. This proves that the intervention of Gods in the successful completion of the mission cannot undermine the bravery of Priam's initiatives. Hermes also expresses his astonishment seeing the old man's intrusion upon such an inimical point along with such valuable treasure. Priam reaches the Achaean camp and crouches at the feet of his enemy, begging for the mercy of the body of his deceased son. Kissing Achilles's hand, he implores him with the long speech –

> "Ah think, thou favour'd of the powers divine!
> Think of thy father's age, and pity mine!
> In me that father's reverend image trace,
> Those silver hairs, that venerable face;
> His trembling limbs, his helpless person, see!
> In all my equal, but in misery!
> Yet now, perhaps, some turn of human fate
> Expels him helpless from his peaceful state;
> Think, from some powerful foe thou seest him fly,
> And beg protection with a feeble cry.
> Yet still one comfort in his soul may rise;
> He hears his son still lives to glad his eyes,
> And, hearing, still may hope a better day
> May send him thee, to chase that foe away.
> No comfort to my griefs, no hopes remain,
> The best, the bravest, of my sons are slain!
> Yet what a race! Ere Greece to Ilion came,
> The pledge of many a loved and loving dame:
> Nineteen one mother bore—Dead, all are dead!"
> ...
> "Think of thy father, and this face behold!
> See him in me, as helpless and as old!
> Though not so wretched: there he yields to me,
> The first of men in sovereign misery!
> Thus forced to kneel, thus grovelling to embrace
> The scourge and ruin of my realm and race;

Suppliant my children's murderer to implore,
And kiss those hands yet reeking with their gore!" (Homer a 729)

This unbelievable courage of Priam shocks Achilles, who has been lamenting the death of Patroclus at the very moment. Homer has given a pitiable description of Priam here –

Unhappy man! Whose death our hands shall grace,
Fate calls thee hence and finish'd is thy race.
Nor longer check my conquests on the foe;
But, pierced by this, to endless darkness go,
And add one spectre to the realms below! (Homer a 338)

Priam's role as a father immediately reminds Achilles that he has not been able to pay threptra to his own biological father and so he considers Priam as his surrogate father, offering him his tribute as a father-substitute. Achilles also gives him protection in the form of a twelve-day truce, while the entire city of Troy has been performing burial rites for Hector. Louise Pratt, seeing the altruistic love of Priam for Hector, opined – "through his act above all, the Iliad suggests that self-sacrifice out of love, the kind associated in the poem with parents, is sufficient in itself, that the investment that ... parents make in their children is worthwhile, even if it is never paid back'." (Pratt 24) The intensity of his paternal love thus has made the impossible possible, and not only that it has also successfully established a sense of closeness with his greatest enemy. K. Crotty described the situation as "the father looms large in the climactic encounter of Priam and Achilles: Priam is moved to supplicate by his fatherly feelings for Hector, and in appealing to Achilles, he expressly invokes the memory of Peleus, Achilles' father". (Crotty 32) Priam and Hector thus depict a positive pattern of father-son bond, though the heroic code of conduct of a king terribly suffers as Priam faces difficulties with mitigating the conflict between his parental role on one hand and his royal roles on the other hand, but *Iliad* defines him with the fatherly quality, setting aside his royal identity.

This fatherly image of Priam can also be evinced in his son Hector from his communication with his son Astyanax. The end of *Book 6* of *Iliad* features a memorable scene in which Hector, the greatest Trojan warrior, bids farewell to his wife Andromache and his son Astyanax as he braces himself to set off for the battle. The parent-child bond as portrayed in the scene exerts its importance in a number of ways. Primarily, it explores the basic similarity between both the ancient and modern idea of considering a child to be the parent's love object, and at the same time, it displays the act of parenting as an activity of love accompanied by attentive caregiving. Several ancient European works depicted that modern concept of parenting is a later development, which was not evident in earlier societies. Lawrence Stone argued that earlier parents refused to invest the same amount of care and attention on their children unlike the modern parents, but this particular scene proves that the parent-child dynamic was idolised in Greek society as much as it is done now in the modern times. The scene appears to be distinctly memorable for its powerful emotional resonance in rendering the importance of the parent-child theme. Astyanax is probably the only child about whom it is mentioned in the main narrative, though there are indirect references of other children in different speeches or similes in the poem. Another vital implication of the scene lies in the fact that Hector can be delineated as a major parental figure, who has dedicated himself to the care of others so deeply that he can also willingly sacrifice his life for their sake. Homer introduces the baby in the passage with utmost delicacy and tenderness; about which G. S. Kirk commented, "... the sympathetic idea of the child held close to his nurse's breast is deepened in successive words and phrases, each touching and carefully chosen". (Kirk 212) The adjective used in the poem 'beloved' and the simile of a beautiful star assigned to his description claims his speciality. The very name Astyanax given to the child has a special meaning – lord of the city, which illustrates the towering status he holds in the city's heart and in the hope of its future. Hector's instant smile seeing the baby shows his parental response but the description of their farewell given by Homer is heart-breaking and heart-rending –

> Thus having spoke, the illustrious chief of Troy
> Stretch'd his fond arms to clasp the lovely boy.
> The babe clung crying to his nurse's breast,
> Scared at the dazzling helm, and nodding crest.
> With secret pleasure each fond parent smiled,
> And Hector hasted to relieve his child,
> The glittering terrors from his brows unbound,
> And placed the beaming helmet on the ground;
> Then kiss'd the child, and, lifting high in air,
> Thus to the gods preferr'd a father's prayer:
> "O thou! whose glory fills the ethereal throne,
> And all ye deathless powers! protect my son!
> Grant him, like me, to purchase just renown,

To guard the Trojans, to defend the crown,
Against his country's foes the war to wage,
And rise the Hector of the future age!
So when triumphant from successful toils
Of heroes slain he bears the reeking spoils,
Whole hosts may hail him with deserved acclaim,
And say, 'This chief transcends his father's fame:'
While pleased amidst the general shouts of Troy,
His mother's conscious heart o'erflows with joy."
He spoke, and fondly gazing on her charms,
Restored the pleasing burden to her arms;
Soft on her fragrant breast the babe she laid,
Hush'd to repose, and with a smile survey'd. (Homer a 204)

The passage views the parent-child bond as one unit. Though there is mention of a silent nurse, yet the scene makes it clear that she plays the role of a support and is never appointed as a replacement of the two parents, who is described to be holding the baby by turns. The child's cry brings smile to his parents, instead of disgust or annoyance, which can be considered to be a typical Greek response to a child's foible, thereby recognising childhood as a distinct stage in human life. Instead of interpreting Astyanax's tears as a mark of cowardice, he acknowledges it to be a natural and an acceptable marker of childhood. It has been commonly observed that consoling or confronting a child is the sole responsibility of a woman, but surprisingly, here Hector is seen to be comforting his child; he immediately takes off his helmet to stop his cry. He also tosses him to divert his attention and also kisses him to soothe him. He also wishes to see his son as a better warrior than himself, which proves him to be a far more generous patriarch than the primordial fathers like Uranus, Cronus, Zeus and others, who are recounted in various legends to have tried to eliminate their sons always to retain their sovereignty. Hector's prayer for his son thus demonstrates human fathers as more selfless and noble than the divine fathers, who have tried to freeze time to preserve the established hierarchy, while the divine and immortal parents have always ruled out this probability. Unlike the Gods, the mortals have always considered their children's success to be their own both in words and actions. In this context, Nancy Felson considered Homeric epic to be un-Freudian, thereby explaining that a gentle and worthy father will always allow his son to surpass him instead of standing in his way.

Modern scholars have identified a tension between Hector's love for his wife and son and his duty towards his country. If he could control his aggression as a warrior a bit more, perhaps he could have served his family better, but his Troy would certainly fall right in the beginning, which he could not allow, but here it is important to note that Homer has never intended to suggest that Hector had to make a choice between his role as a father and as a king; rather he casts him as a doting father, who has sacrificed his life for others. His failure can never be attributed to his lack of admiration for his son, but he fails because he is not as good as a warrior as compared to Achilles; he is less scheming as compared to Odysseus; and lastly because he lacks any divine power or assistance unlike many other combatants.

In the epic poem, Achilles' relation with his father-figures also serves as eminent sources, exploring the important theme of father-son bonding. Apart from his biological father, the ninth book of *Iliad* mentions about his surrogate and second father Phoenix, although his first appearance is in *Book I.* He appears here along with Agamemnon, Nestor, Odysseus, Ajax, and others to persuade Achilles to participate in the war against the Trojans as the Achaean side is hugely dependent on his skill. When Achilles rejects the plea of both Agamemnon and Odysseus, Phoenix becomes vocal for the first time. By addressing Achilles as his 'dear son', he comforts him, asserting that if he wishes to leave Troy the day after, he will surely accompany him. He further states that when his own father Amyntor curses him to be childless for seducing his father's concubine following his mother's wish, he has taken resort to Phthia, where Peleus receives him warmly and makes him a king of the Dolopian and hands over to him his own son Achilles. From then onwards, he has always treated and loved Achilles as a father. Achilles in his infancy has never even eaten in Phoenix's absence, he used to hold him with his knees, cut his meat, feed him, and give him wine, which would wet his chiton. He always has been Achilles' protector and care-giver. Peleus has sent him to the war as a teacher and so he maintains that he will always stay with him.

> The royal Peleus, when from Pthia's coast
> He sent thee early to the Achaian host;
> Thy youth as then in sage debates unskill'd,
> And new to perils of the direful field:
> He bade me teach thee all the ways of war,
> To shine in councils, and in camps to dare. (Homer a 284)

He also assures him that he will not get separated from him under any circumstances, yet he tries to convince him to eject his anger and enter in the battle before it gets too late. He also proclaims that if Achilles agrees to his proposal, he will be honoured as a God by the Greeks. Even in the most furious state of mind, Achilles reacts to his long speech affectionately and implores him not to take the side of Agamemnon as it can rouse anger in him. The poet here mentioned that Phoenix is to stay in Achilles' camp for the rest of the night in order to provide him comfort. This part of the narrative proclaims Phoenix as Achilles' second father, who can exert emotional pressure to convince him his words, which the others present in the scene is unable or has no right to do.

Peleus, Achilles' biological father, also forms a ripe example of an emotional father in the narrative. The readers get to know from Odysseus' speech that he himself has taken his son to Agamemnon before the Achaean army has started their journey. He has personally given him to Agamemnon, who is the commander-in-chief of the Greeks, and has personally requested him to take care of his son as a father. Here, Odysseus reminds Achilles that disobeying Agamemnon is hence equivalent to disobeying his own father. Even his farewell advice to his son exhibits his care as well as his duty towards his son –

> "My child! With strength, with glory, and success,
> Thy arms may Juno and Minerva bless!
> Trust that to Heaven: but thou, thy cares engage
> To calm thy passions, and subdue thy rage:
> From gentler manners let thy glory grow,
> And shun contention, the sure source of woe;
> That young and old may in thy praise combine,
> The virtues of humanity be thine—'
> This now-despised advice thy father gave;
> Ah! Check thy anger; and be truly brave..." (Homer a 274)

The character of Patroclus in the epic poem features confusion in the narrative. Undoubtedly, his death instantly settles down the wrath of Achilles, which gets substituted by revenge and he returns to the battle without a second thought. Absolutely like Phoenix, Peleus gives shelter to Patroclus as well when his father Menoetius sends him to Phthia after he kills another child in anger over a game. Peleus treats both Phoenix and Patroclus as his own sons and shares his fatherly responsibility of nurturing and raising Achilles with them. Patroclus is much younger to Phoenix in age but he is older than Achilles and hence he is both an elder brother and a father to Achilles. Peleus has entrusted both Achilles and Patroclus to Agamemnon as if to be a substitute of him. It can be interpreted from the description that Patroclus serves the function of being the doublet, better, or alter ego of Achilles, though from the words of his biological father Menoetius, it can be deduced that he is the weaker counterpart of Achilles. They have grown up together as brothers and even when Nestor and Odysseus arrive to seek for war participants, they have spotted them together. Though Patroclus was never a match to Achilles' skill, yet his exceptional judgemental power compels Achilles to assign him two most important tasks of his life. He knows that he is not destined to return from the Trojan War, but Peleus in his old age must be perishing with sorrow and so he has always counted on Patroclus that he will be taking care of his kin and property in Phthia. In *Book 19*, Briseis after the death of Patroclus grieves revealing that he has promised her to make her the legally wedded wife of Achilles, once they return to Phthia after the battle ends. Thus, Patroclus is a matchmaker as well as a guardian to Achilles, who is supposed to secure the continuity of the generations and serve as a father and household to his heir Neoptolemus, but all his hopes turn to despair at Patroclus' death and he recounts with a sigh –

> "Thou too, Patroclus! (thus his heart he vents)
> Once spread the inviting banquet in our tents:
> Thy sweet society, thy winning care,
> Once stay'd Achilles, rushing to the war.
> But now, alas! To death's cold arms resign'd,
> What banquet but revenge can glad my mind?
> What greater sorrow could afflict my breast,
> What more if hoary Peleus were deceased?
> Who now, perhaps, in Phthia dreads to hear
> His son's sad fate, and drops a tender tear.
> What more, should Neoptolemus the brave,
> My only offspring, sink into the grave?
> If yet that offspring lives; (I distant far,
> Of all neglectful, wage a hateful war.)
> I could not this, this cruel stroke attend;
> Fate claim'd Achilles, but might spare his friend.
> I hoped Patroclus might survive, to rear
> My tender orphan with a parent's care,
> From Scyros' isle conduct him o'er the main,
> And glad his eyes with his paternal reign,

The lofty palace, and the large domain.
For Peleus breathes no more the vital air;
Or drags a wretched life of age and care,
But till the news of my sad fate invades
His hastening soul, and sinks him to the shades." (Homer a 587)

Peleus vows that after his son returns home from the war, he will make him sacrifice his hair to a Phthian river Sperchios and it has been seen that Achilles commemorates his filial bond with his dead friend Patroclus in his funeral by cutting his hair. In this act, Achilles equates the death of Patroclus with the death of his biological father Peleus. He mourns the fact that he has become the reason of both their deaths unwillingly. Peleus will surely die on the very day, he hears that his son has been killed while Patroclus had to lose his life in the battlefield since Achilles refuses to take part in the battle anymore and hence he had to participate in the war in place of Achilles. Had Achilles not fought over a woman with Agamemnon, Patroclus would have been alive. He holds himself responsible for both their destructions. Patroclus' death haunts Achilles with the horror of a patricide, considering him to be his father substitute.

All night Achilles hails Patroclus' soul,
With large libations from the golden bowl.
As a poor father, helpless and undone,
Mourns o'er the ashes of an only son,
Takes a sad pleasure the last bones to burn,
And pours in tears, ere yet they close the urn:
So stay'd Achilles, circling round the shore,
So watch'd the flames, till now they flame no more.
'Twas when, emerging through the shades of night. (Homer a 678)

In the Trojan War, the divine fathers are evinced to display a very different kind of bond with their sons, which are never earlier witnessed. Sarpedon is introduced by Homer in the epic as a Lycian prince, who is one of the main heroes during the battle, fighting on the side of the Troy. He is known to be the son of Apollo and Laodameia and the cousin of Glaucus of Lycia, the second-in-command of the Lycian army. Sarpedon leading Lycian forces are considered to be the most powerful allies of the Troy and hence he is regarded as the greatest defender of the Trojan force and almost equivalent to Hector and Aeneas. His cousin and son of Hippolochus, Glaucus, starts off for the battle from Xanthos with Sarpedon, where Glaucus meets Diomedes, who is supposedly the leader of the Greek forces aided by Goddess Athena. In the battlefield, Glaucus and Diomedes, while exchanging words with each other, come to know about each other's ancestors; both their grandfathers coincidentally have been close friends and this information compels them to agree on one point that they will carry forward the tradition of friendship by gifting each other their armours and so they will never fight with each other in spite of being on opposing sides. Meanwhile, Sarpedon defeats and kills Tlepolemus, who manages to injure him in the left thigh. He also with the help of his cousin and Asteropaeus, another Trojan ally, helps Hector to breach the defences of the Greeks by storming the Greek fortifications. His influence in the war is so important and overpowering that on one occasion he even criticizes Hector, accusing him of leaving the fight for the Trojan allies instead of directing the Trojan forces themselves to actively participate in the war.

When following the fight between Achilles and Agamemnon, Patroclus fights as a substitute to Achilles, Sarpedon meets him in a duel. Apollo, predicting the fate which is destined to befall on Sarpedon, attempts to remove him from the battlefield, but Hera warns him that the other Olympian deities will certainly object to the divine intervention as many of their own mortal children themselves are participants in the war. Apollo has no other choice but to comply to their demur, but at the same time he ensures that his body has to be send to Lycia after his death by the hands of Patroclus. Jove commands Phoebus, Apollo's chief epithet –

> "Descend, my Phoebus! On the Phrygian plain,
> And from the fight convey Sarpedon slain;
> Then bathe his body in the crystal flood,
> With dust dishonour'd, and deform'd with blood;
> O'er all his limbs ambrosial odours shed,
> And with celestial robes adorn the dead.
> Those rites discharged, his sacred corse bequeath
> To the soft arms of silent Sleep and Death.
> They to his friends the immortal charge shall bear;
> His friends a tomb and pyramid shall rear:
> What honour mortals after death receive,
> Those unavailing honours we may give!" (Homer a 502)

The death of the God-like hero follows a fierce fight as both the sides claim the body. Just as the Trojans picks his armour, Apollo appears with Hypnos (Sleep) and Thanatos (Death) to purify the body with ambrosia and take it back to Lycia. During the fight, he is recounted to shower bloody raindrops over the Trojans, which expresses his grief for the impending death of his mortal son.

In case of Neleus and Nestor as a father and son, they have not got enough opportunities to relish their bond. Nestor plays the role of a wise advisor in *Iliad*, who motivates the warriors with his paradigmatic tales. While persuading Patroclus to convince Achilles to return to the battlefield, he recounts the caring paternal attitude of his own father Neleus towards him. He begins by informing Patroclus that, much before the Trojan War, he originally hails from a place called Gerenia, where he had been counted as an Argonaut, a band of heroes, who accompanied Jason to seek the Golden Fleece. In the mission, he had to fight the centaurs, whose upper body was that of a human and lower body and legs of a horse. He also took part in hunting the Calydonian Boar. He further illustrates a war between Pylos and Elis, where at one point Pylos got impoverished and weakened; all the best Pylian warriors were killed and the Elean folks continued their attack and violence. They also directed their insults towards Neleus, which was too much for Nestor to bear. All of Neleus' sons were already killed in the battle, except Nestor, and so it was his responsibility to come to the rescue of the Pylian people. He instantly administered a successful raid against the Eleans, killing one of the chieftains. Soon, the Elean force started their counter-attack. Nestor performed marvellously, thereby routing their enemies completely. But in this tale, we find a father who, very similar to Priam, casting off his royal persona, gets stressed at the thought of losing his only surviving son. He tries to resist him from participating in the battle by adopting different strategies. He had hid his son's horses, considering him too young to fight the enemy, but this did not prevent Nestor from going in the battlefield; he set off on foot and slayed the Elean Itymoneus (the son of Hypeirochus) with a spear and Mulius (the son-in-law of Augeas) and thus made his father proud and also saved his honour at the same time.

"Can then the sons of Greece (the sage rejoin'd)
Excite compassion in Achilles' mind?
Seeks he the sorrows of our host to know?
This is not half the story of our woe.
Tell him, not great Machaon bleeds alone,
Our bravest heroes in the navy groan,
Ulysses, Agamemnon, Diomed,
And stern Eurypylus, already bleed.
But, ah! What flattering hopes I entertain!

Achilles heeds not, but derides our pain:
Even till the flames consume our fleet he stays,
And waits the rising of the fatal blaze.
Chief after chief the raging foe destroys;
Calm he looks on, and every death enjoys.
Now the slow course of all-impairing time
Unstrings my nerves, and ends my manly prime;
Oh! Had I still that strength my youth possess'd,
When this bold arm the Epeian powers oppress'd,
The bulls of Elis in glad triumph led,
And stretch'd the great Itymonaeus dead!
Then from my fury fled the trembling swains,
And ours was all the plunder of the plains:
Fifty white flocks, full fifty herds of swine,
As many goats, as many lowing kine:
And thrice the number of unrivall'd steeds,
All teeming females, and of generous breeds.
These, as my first essay of arms, I won;
Old Neleus gloried in his conquering son.
Thus Elis forced, her long arrears restored,
And shares were parted to each Pylian lord.
The state of Pyle was sunk to last despair,
When the proud Elians first commenced the war:
For Neleus' sons Alcides' rage had slain;
Of twelve bold brothers, I alone remain!
Oppress'd, we arm'd; and now this conquest gain'd,
My sire three hundred chosen sheep obtain'd.
(That large reprisal he might justly claim,
For prize defrauded, and insulted fame,
When Elis' monarch, at the public course,
Detain'd his chariot, and victorious horse.)
The rest the people shared; myself survey'd
The just partition, and due victims paid.
Three days were past, when Elis rose to war,
With many a courser, and with many a car;
The sons of Actor at their army's head
(Young as they were) the vengeful squadrons led.
High on the rock fair Thryoessa stands,
Our utmost frontier on the Pylian lands:
Not far the streams of famed Alphaeus flow:

> The stream they pass'd, and pitch'd their tents below.
> Pallas, descending in the shades of night,
> Alarms the Pylians and commands the fight.
> Each burns for fame, and swells with martial pride,
> Myself the foremost; but my sire denied;
> Fear'd for my youth, exposed to stern alarms;
> And stopp'd my chariot, and detain'd my arms.
> My sire denied in vain: on foot I fled
> Amidst our chariots; for the goddess led. (Homer a 346)

The Homeric society is thus fundamentally featured with the relationships between fathers and sons. The war heroes of *Iliad* are basically identified by their filial status as Achilles, often addressed as 'son of Peleus' (or Peleides), while Agamemnon is called the 'son of Atreus' (or Atreides). The patriarchal household forms the basic structure of the society and the image of the household shaped the communal institutions. Zeus, being the monarch of the Olympus, is approached as 'the father of the Gods', whereas Agamemnon tends to perform the role of a patriarch of the Achaean princes in the epic poem, thereby displaying 'the sceptre of his fathers' to indicate his authority. The power of filial affection anchored individual loyalty to communal duty, while fatherhood and nobility demonstrates modes of continuity as opposed to mutability and morality. The dignity and melancholy of fatherhood form the backdrop of the Trojan War – Apollo sobbing for Sarpedon, Neleus' anxiety for Nestor, Hector's farewell to Astyanax, Priam's apprehension for Hector and later mourning his death, and Peleus perturbation while sending Achilles to aid the Achaeans are all proofs of this. Thomas Greene in *The Descent from Heaven* concluded that *Iliad* is "a great poem of fatherhood" (Greene 7).

The mothers in the poem are also not very dissimilar to the fathers in taking responsibilities of their sons' victory or in showing concern for them. As earlier mentioned, Hecuba consistently tries to debar Hector from facing Achilles, while Thetis aids her son Achilles by gifting him armour made by Hephaestus, which will protect her son from any mortal wound. Other divine mothers mentioned in the narrative include Iris, the mother of Aeneas and Hera, the mother of Hephaestus.

Women in the ancient texts have not only served the roles of being wives or daughters of heroes or villains but have also been assigned important tasks as their mothers. Queen Hecuba is best known in *Iliad* as the mother of both Hector and Paris. Her motherly persona gets prominent when she begs Hector not to participate in the war against Achilles, to which he refuses to pay any heed as usual –

> "O Hector! Say, what great occasion calls
> My son from fight, when Greece surrounds our walls;
> Com'st thou to supplicate the almighty power
> With lifted hands, from Ilion's lofty tower?
> Stay, till I bring the cup with Bacchus crown'd,
> In Jove's high name, to sprinkle on the ground,
> And pay due vows to all the gods around.
> Then with a plenteous draught refresh thy soul,
> And draw new spirits from the generous bowl;
> Spent as thou art with long laborious fight,
> The brave defender of thy country's right." (Homer a 193)

She also gathers a number of Trojan women to offer a treasured gown to satisfy Athena so that she keeps Troy safe from the Achaean forces. As a mother, Hecuba never steps back to do anything to protect her sons. In spite of being the Queen of Troy, she readily serves as a slave to the Greek hero Odysseus, when he journeys it through Thrace, ruled by King Polymestor, whom she urges to protect her son Polydorus, but upon reaching Thrace, to her utter dismay, she discovers that the king has already killed the boy. This enrages Hecuba so much that she gets furious and tears out Polymestor's eyes and also murders his two sons. Odysseus attempts to control her but in vain. She turns herself into a dog in rage.

The epic poem celebrates motherhood through the role of another very important divine mother, the sea Goddess Thetis, who plays a very eminent part in the war as a pillar of support for his son Achilles. On various occasions in the narrative, the readers come to witness her motherly affection. Thetis gives birth to his son with a mortal king Peleus, whom she marries at the command of Zeus. Achilles being a mortal son is doomed to survive for a little span of time on earth, and knowing that he is fated to die young, Thetis desperately makes several attempts to protect her son, thereby trying to grant him immortality denied by his human heritage. In his infancy, she has fed Achilles the food of the Gods, ambrosia and has laid him in the holy fire every night to burn away his mortality, but all her best efforts prove to be ineffective. Nevertheless, she never gives up her endeavour. She takes the child to River Styx and dips him in the waters, trying to infuse him with immortality. This time she gets partially successful. While dipping him in the holy water, she holds him by his heel, which remains outside water and hence this part of his body remains mortal and vulnerable and will be responsible for his death in his later life.

Again, Thetis proves her motherly obsession when she gets to know about the Trojan War, where Achilles will play a very important role in it and is destined to die. She immediately sends him to the court of Lycomedes on the island of Skyros as an attempt to conceal him in order to prevent him from participating in the war. Her effort fails when the Greek warrior Odysseus instead of being fooled himself, tricks Achilles into revealing himself. Immediately, without wasting time, she goes to seek the help of Hephaestus and pleads him to craft a set of Godly armour for her son, which will protect him in the battle, but unfortunately the narrative discloses that the very armour proves to be the prime reason for his downfall as when he gifts it to his beloved Patroclus, it gives him an inflated sense of confidence, which further leads him to his doom. Patroclus' death shocks Achilles and this instigates him to decide to avenge his death at any cost. This terrifies his protective mother, who very similar to Queen Hecuba, urges Achilles not to participate in the war with Hector and live a long peaceful life by accepting his fate, but just like Hector he ignores her plea, though unlike Hector, he emerges as a winner in this particular duel. This outstanding victory of Achilles is not only due to his skill alone, but it cannot be denied that Thetis' ardent prayer to all the Gods has borne the unbelievable magnificent result –

> "O thou supreme! High-throned all height above!
> O great Pelasgic, Dodonaean Jove!
> Who 'midst surrounding frosts, and vapours chill,
> Presid'st on bleak Dodona's vocal hill:
> (Whose groves the Selli, race austere! Surround,
> Their feet unwash'd, their slumbers on the ground;
> Who hear, from rustling oaks, thy dark decrees;
> And catch the fates, low-whispered in the breeze;)
> Hear, as of old! Thou gav'st, at Thetis' prayer,
> Glory to me, and to the Greeks despair.
> Lo, to the dangers of the fighting field
> The best, the dearest of my friends, I yield,
> Though still determined, to my ships confined;
> Patroclus gone, I stay but half behind.
> Oh! Be his guard thy providential care,
> Confirm his heart, and string his arm to war:
> Press'd by his single force let Hector see

His fame in arms not owing all to me.
But when the fleets are saved from foes and fire,
Let him with conquest and renown retire;
Preserve his arms, preserve his social train,
And safe return him to these eyes again!" (Homer a 484)

Hector's defeat has not alone satisfied Achilles; his rage has not yet been reduced. He hitches the dead body of Hector with his chariot and drags it around the city, thereby refusing to allow the Trojans to arrange a proper burial for him. This disregard for burial rites enrages the Gods, who implore Thetis to warn his son against this behaviour. Soon, Thetis appears in front of Achilles to stop him from his irrational action to safeguard him from the wrath of the Gods. In this manner, the readers can find Thetis playing the role of an obsessed mother on various occasions, concentrating only on one purpose – the defence of her son from any kind of unwanted consequences.

The other mother-son duo that features in *Iliad* is Aphrodite and Aineías. He is named by his mother; the word referring to 'terrible grief'. While naming her son, Aphrodite keeps on thinking of the immense sorrow that she had to suffer due to him. Zeus has been enraged with Aphrodite on the fact that she has made the Greek Gods fall in love with the mortals and hence he punishes her by making her fall in love with Anchises, who gets mesmerized by her beauty. She warns him not to disclose their association to anyone, but Anchises fails to keep his words; the moment he reveals the name of the mother of his son, he is struck with lightening and is possibly killed. Aineías is a minor character in the war, but he has played an important role in defending against the Achaean enemy during the Trojan War.

Aphrodite has played a very important role as a mother in the war. She has been spotted more than once to help her son escape unfavourable situations. On one occasion, in a combat with Diomedes of Argos, Aineías gets almost slain, but Aphrodite, with the help of Apollo, heals him by taking him to Pergamos, a Turkish Cypriot village.

In contrast to other mothers and sons, Hera and Hephaestus share a very controversial relationship as a mother and son. While taking his birth, Hephaestus' parents, Apollo and Hera, get enraged in a brawl and in disgust both of them cast him from heaven one by one. To take revenge, Hephaestus crafts a magical golden throne for his mother, upon which she seats and gets stuck to it. Seeing her pitiful condition, all the other Gods plead to Hephaestus to let her go, advocating on behalf of Hera. He sulkily proclaims that he has no mother, but at the same time he has been seen in the epic poem to settle an argument between Apollo and Hera by asking Hera to accept a goblet of wine to calm her own self and thus to aid the Gods to work together peacefully.

The character of Andromache also forms a suiting example of a dedicated and concerned mother. While introducing herself, she never forgets to mention being the mother of Astyanax, besides defining herself as the wife of the famous warrior Hector. On receiving the news of Hector's death, she worries for her son's future, predicting that he must be deprived of luxury and love in absence of his father. Her words speak the mother in her –

An only child, once comfort of my pains,
Sad product now of hapless love, remains!
No more to smile upon his sire; no friend
To help him now! No father to defend!
For should he 'scape the sword, the common doom,
What wrongs attend him, and what griefs to come!
Even from his own paternal roof expell'd,
Some stranger ploughs his patrimonial field.
The day, that to the shades the father sends,
Robs the sad orphan of his father's friends:
He, wretched outcast of mankind! Appears
For ever sad, for ever bathed in tears;
Amongst the happy, unregarded, he
Hangs on the robe, or trembles at the knee,
While those his father's former bounty fed
Nor reach the goblet, nor divide the bread:
The kindest but his present wants allay,
To leave him wretched the succeeding day.
Frugal compassion! Heedless, they who boast
Both parents still, nor feel what he has lost,
Shall cry, 'Begone! Thy father feasts not here:'
The wretch obeys, retiring with a tear.
Thus wretched, thus retiring all in tears,
To my sad soul Astyanax appears!
Forced by repeated insults to return,
And to his widow'd mother vainly mourn:
He, who, with tender delicacy bred,
With princes sported, and on dainties fed,

And when still evening gave him up to rest,
Sunk soft in down upon the nurse's breast,
Must—ah what must he not? Whom Ilion calls
Astyanax, from her well-guarded walls,
Is now that name no more, unhappy boy!
Since now no more thy father guards his Troy. (Homer a 665)

The epic poem of Homer thus presents with many examples of the Jungian psychologist Erich Neumann's 'Great mother', who can fight the Gods and at same time satisfy them for the cause of their children.

Parent-child dynamics especially father-son relationship features yet in another important epic poem of Homer, *Odyssey*, which recounts the tale of Odysseus, the king of Ithaca, who is known to wander for ten years before returning home from the Trojan War. The twenty-four books of the epic begin in the middle of the story, narrating various incidents, which has already occurred in the past through the voice of Odysseus himself. The series begins with a large rowdy mob of suitors, who in absence of the king, have overrun the palace of Ithaca and ravaged the city, and are now waiting to court the Queen of Ithaca and Odysseus' wife Penelope, but she gives her whole effort to remain loyal to her husband. Odysseus's son Prince Telemachus desperately tries to rescue and protect her mother from the suitors, but he lacks confidence and experience to encounter them. Being unsure of the fact that Odysseus is still alive, Antinous, one of the suitors, plots to assassinate the young prince to get rid of the only opposition of their dominion over both the queen and the palace.

Meanwhile, Odysseus is imprisoned by a beautiful nymph Calypso, possessed by her love, on her island Ogygia. He tries to escape from her as he yearns to see his family, but he is bereft of his ship and crew who could have saved him from the situation. This initiates a debate among the deities of the Mount Olympus regarding Odysseus' future. His strongest defender among them Athena decides to aid Telemachus in his effort. She disguises herself as a friend of Laertes, Telemachus' grandfather, and persuades him to call a meeting of the assembly, in which he is about to approach the suitors. Athena helps him prepare for a journey to Pylos and Sparta, where he would meet Odysseus' companions, Nestor and Menelaus, who will inform him of Odysseus' current state. After the plan of Athena gets accomplished and Telemachus learns about the imprisonment of Odysseus on Calypso's island, he decides to return home to Ithaca, where Antinous waits with other suitors, preparing an ambush to kill him the moment he reaches the port.

Apollo finally comes to the rescue of the homesick Odysseus by sending Hermes to Calypso to convince her to allow Odysseus to build a ship and leave for Ithaca. This time the God of the Sea Poseidon creates a hindrance by sending a fearful storm to wreck his ship, thereby avenging his son, the Cyclops Polyphemus' blindness, caused by Odysseus' earlier rage. Athena again comes to his rescue. She calms Poseidon and saves the beleaguered king by helping him at Scheria, which is the home of the Phaeacians. The Phaeacian princess Nausica escorts him to her palace, where both the king and the queen welcome him warmly. When they learn that he is Odysseus, they promise to help him return to his home after hearing the stories of his adventures. Odysseus heeds to their request. He narrates the incidents that he has experienced on Calypso's island and in the land of Lotus Eaters as well as he describes his duel with Polyphemus the Cyclops; his courtship with Circe, the witch-goddess; his temptations by the deadly Sirens; his voyage to Hades to seek the advice of the prophet Tiresias; and lastly, his battle with the sea monster Scylla. At last after fulfilling the wish of the Phaeacian king and queen, he safely returns home finally with their assistance, but in disguise of a beggar, as directed by Athena. Nevertheless, his faithful swineherd Eumaeus receives him warmly in his own hut and serves him food. Very soon, he reveals his identity to his son Telemachus, who has returned from Pylos and Sparta shortly and has luckily escaped from the suitors' ambush. They both make a plan immediately to rescue Ithaca from the control of the suitors, thereby regaining all that is their own.

The following day, according to the plan, Odysseus, still disguised as a beggar, returns to the palace, where he receives humiliation and abuses from the suitors. None except Eurycleia, his old nurse, recognises him, but she promises to keep his identity a secret from the rest. Penelope, unable to bear any more, arranges an archery contest and declares that the one who can string her husband's great bow and fire an arrow through a row of twelve axes will surely win her and get a chance to marry her. This feat seems impossible for all except Odysseus himself. Each and every suitor fails in their attempt as expected; just then Odysseus in the appearance of a beggar steps forward and easily completes the task with little effort. He instantly turns the great bow on the suitors and successfully kills everyone with the help of his son and a few faithful servants.

Odysseus finally unveils his true identity, thereby reuniting with his beloved wife. The very next day, he goes to the outskirts of the city to meet with his aging father, where he further gets attacked by the family members of the dead suitors though Laertes helps him to overcome them, especially the father of Antinous. The long poem thus ends with Apollo appointing Athena to restore peace in Ithaca with the whole family getting reunited after a very long time.

Very similar to *Iliad*, *Odyssey* also engages its readers with the motifs of the father-son bond; the entire plot of action is connected to the theme of family and its importance as a well-balanced unit. The father-son pairs which draw special attention include Odysseus and Telemachus, Odysseus and his father Laertes, Nestor and Pisistratus, Poseidon and the Cyclops Polyphemus, and Eupithes and Antinous, who contribute in maintaining the continuity between the generations either for good or evil. The epic poem also highlights the fact that a strong family bond can easily aid in overcoming impossible odds.

The evolution of a family having the focal point in the fathers-son relationship is featured in the last few books of *Odyssey*. Telemachus, the son of Odysseus, is first introduced by Athena while she outlines her plan for his future even before he truly appears in the action. Even in the absence of his father, he is seen to defend his father's name and thus on several occasions, he participates in the hanging of the servant, who is found betraying his father's trust. In their long separation, they have both missed each other and have dreamt of getting reunited someday. Telemachus in the poem recounts about his father in his absence using various adjectives like noble and god-like, though he has never seen his father since he has been born. Odysseus has left Ithaca just after Telemachus' birth and so they never have got an opportunity to demonstrate love and care for one another, yet they have always longed to meet each other. It is through distance that they seem to grow love and admiration for each other; rather this physical distance helps them to cement their bond. Homer's description of their reunion thus speaks about the longing for each other –

> ... Telemachus threw his arms
> around his great father, sobbing uncontrollably
> as the deep desire for tears welled up in both.
> They cried out, shrilling cries, pulsing sharper
> than birds of prey—eagles, vultures with hooked claws—
> when farmers plunder their nest of young too young to fly.
> Both men so filled with compassion, eyes streaming tears,
> that now the sunlight would have set upon their cries
> If Telemachus had not asked his father, all at once,
> "What sort of ship, dear father, brought you here?—
> Ithaca, at last. Who did the sailors say they are?
> I hardly think you came back home on foot!" (Homer b 271)

Being the son of Odysseus, he is expected to possess the god-like traits of his father such as a strong sense of hospitality, loyalty towards his subjects, intelligence, and patience, along with other impeccable manners. He has all these qualities but nevertheless he fails to manage the household successfully especially in presence of the guests, where his behaviour is unexpectedly odd. This obliges Athena to send him on a quest, where he can gather some information about his father and at the same time, he can acquire some knowledge which will help him to substitute his father competently.

Telemachus, following the instruction of Athena, sets off on his voyage, where he first encounters with Nestor and then with Menelaus, who provide him with the exact illustration of a healthy fathers-son dynamic, which serves as an indoctrination of the manners and behaviours required to be a successful heir to a father of his rank. He finally learns to stand by his father in outwitting and outfighting the uninvited guests, being the replica of his father and thus restoring peace and prosperity in Ithaca.

The main protagonist of the epic poem Odysseus re-encounters with his son Telemachus almost after twenty years. They have spent a very long time without each other, undergoing trials and hardships that poise them for their final confrontation. Both the father and the son arrive almost around the same time on the island of Ithaca and seek shelter in the swineherd's security. Odysseus, in disguise of the beggar, seems to be dominant in offering his seat to the prince, who refuses the offer chivalrously, and in this act, they display their humility and likeness to each other.

Homer prescribed the same kind of loyalty and love in the relationship between Odysseus and his father Laertes, thus foregrounding the necessity of retaining continuity between generations in order to maintain peace in the household and find success in kingship. After the departure of his son Odysseus from Ithaca, Laertes loses all the strength and ability of being a ruler in lieu of being away from his son. He transforms into a commoner, thus neglecting his duty towards his grandson and daughter-in-law. Similarly, Odysseus also grieves for his father's company and longs to see him. The moment he returns to his motherland, he goes to see his father though being in disguise of a beggar. It gets difficult for him to hide his true identity from his father, who is suffering pitifully in absence of his son. At last, he reveals his true self by exhibiting the tree, which he gave him in his childhood – a symbol of inheritance, and a scar, which helps them to get reunited immediately. Laertes, finally getting his son back, regains his strength with the help of Athena and agrees to reclaim the kingdom of Ithaca to be his own.

Telemachus encounters Nestor in the palace of Pylos surrounded by his son preparing for a huge celebration in the honour of Poseidon. For the first time in his life, he witnesses a father-son bond, where Nestor treats his sons as like-minded companions, and at the same time, plays the role of a guide to them. This fascinates Telemachus very much as he has always been bereft of the physical presence of his father. Besides being a friend to his sons, Nestor also gives them full freedom to decide the course of their way of life. He sets different goals for them by assigning them different tasks like arranging huge feast, but at the same time, he allows them to choose their own methods of accomplishing them. Nestor calls out –

> "Quickly, my children, carry out my wishes now
> so I may please the gods, Athena first of all—
> she came to me at Poseidon's flowing feast,
> Athena in all her glory!
> Now someone go to the fields to fetch a heifer,
> lead her here at once—a herdsman drive her in.
> Someone hurry down to Prince Telemachus' black ship,
> bring up all his crewmen, leave just two behind.
> And another tell our goldsmith, skilled Laerces,
> to come and sheathe the heifer's horns in gold.
> The rest stay here together. Tell the maids
> inside the hall to prepare a sumptuous feast—
> bring seats and firewood, bring pure water too." (Homer b 47)

Peisistratus, his youngest son, following Nestor's instruction, provides horses and a chariot and accompanies Telemachus to visit Menelaus in Sparta, where he comes across another father, though here he sees the sons taking no part in hospitality in receiving the guests of the household, unlike the case of Nestor's palace. Menelaus does not have any male heir with Helen, but he is fond of his two sons by the slave women, Megapenthes and Nicostratus. He even makes his illegitimate son Megapenthes his heir. Thus, both the palaces of Nestor as well as Menelaus give Telemachus an opportunity to observe father-figures, which provides him a model to emulate and also helps him to become a better and more responsible adult. One can also find other desperate fathers like Poseidon and Eupithes, who avenges their sons' blindness and death respectively by launching an attack on Odysseus, without fearing about the consequences of their actions.

Odysseus, besides providing its readers a number of committed fathers, also presents an exceedingly devoted mother Penelope, who single-handedly nurtures his son Telemachus for twenty long years. In absence of her husband, being a single mother, she plays both the roles of a mother as well as a father. She introduces her son to his father through stories and successfully begets respect in him for his father even when he has never seen him physically for such a long period of time. It is solely due to her that Telemachus emulates his father in showing hospitality, loyalty, and patience towards his subjects. Similarly, Telemachus is gifted with another mother-figure, his nurse Eurycleia, who has always cared for him and helped Penelope in begetting Telemachus. Eurycleia is brought by Odysseus' father Laertes and is always treated by him as his wife, but she has refused to consummate him as a lover and decides to stay as a nurse of Odysseus, so as not to disrespect Laertes' real wife Anticleia. Her motherly dedication and care are well assorted in Homer's description of her –

> She was his grandson's escort now and bore a torch,
> for she was the one of all the maids who loved
> the prince the most—she'd nursed him as a baby.
> He spread the doors of his snug, well-made room,
> sat down on the bed and pulled his soft shirt off,
> tossed it into the old woman's conscientious hands,
> and after folding it neatly, patting it smooth,
> she hung it up on a peg beside his corded bed,
> then padded from the bedroom,
> drawing the door shut with the silver hook,
> sliding the doorbolt home with its rawhide strap. (Homer b 18)

Penelope has always remained worried about Odysseus' return, especially being always under the pressure of her suitors. As her son steps into adolescence, she assumes a subordinate position in the household, thereby allowing or rather pushing her son to become a man of the house and order his mother around. The insecure and lonely mother in her cries out hearing that Telemachus has decided to go for a voyage in order to seek information of his father –

> "Oh herald, why has my child gone and left me?
> No need in the world for him to board the ships,
> Those chariots of the sea that sweep men on,
> Driving across the ocean's endless wastes …
> Does he want his very name wiped off the earth?" (Homer b 73)

She has almost lost her husband but she cannot take any chance with his son. Telemachus, being inexperienced and young, tries his best to safeguard his mother from the hostile suitors but fails to manage them alone.

Goddess Athena has always been a divine patron to Odysseus, protecting him from all dangers. Even in the absence of Odysseus, Athena disguises herself as Mentes and comes to guide Telemachus as a father-substitute. Telemachus himself finds a father in Mentes, which can be easily learnt from their conversation when he proclaims –

> "Oh stranger,"
> heedful Telemachus replied, "indeed I will.
> You've counseled me with so much kindness now,
> like a father to a son. I won't forget a word.
> But come, stay longer, keen as you are to sail,
> so you can bathe and rest and lift your spirits,
> then go back to your ship, delighted with a gift,
> a prize of honor, something rare and fine
> as a keepsake from myself. The kind of gift
> a host will give a stranger, friend to friend." (Homer b 156)

In the exhibition of masculinity, Homeric epics have always displayed a father's act of sharing the centre stage with his young son. A gentle and loving father guides his son to perform his duties and a responsible son always sustains his parents in old age as a repayment of their nurturing. Often death has acted as a hindrance, thereby debarring unfortunate parents from getting their share of threptra from their biological sons. Hector has died young and is unable to pay threptra to his father Priam, but Achilles, his greatest enemy, fulfils Hector's duty by paying threptra to Priam, which he is unable to pay to his true father. Other warriors like Sinoeisius and Hippothus have died before their parents and hence cannot repay their due.

Hesiod had introduced a new word for the whole idea of threptra, 'threpteria', having a slightly different meaning, i.e., the obligation of giving reward by children to their parents for their rearing. He describes the laborious and sorrowful fifth age, claiming –

> And Zeus will destroy this race of mortal men also when they come to have grey hair on the temples at their birth. The father will not agree with his children, nor the children with their father, nor guest with his host, nor comrade with comrade; nor will brother be dear to brother as aforetime. Men will dishonor their parents as they grow quickly old,

> and will carp at them, chiding them with bitter words, hard-hearted they, not knowing the fear of the gods. They will not repay their aged parents the cost of their nurture, for might shall be their right: and one man will sack another's city. (Hesiod 174)

The passage describes how the moral character of the men of the fifth age has suffered deterioration. *Oedipus at Colonus* is said to be set in this period of immorality, which specially features the decline of familial relationships. Polynices and Eteocles, the two sons of Oedipus, have been busy fighting for kingship, instead of taking care of their blind and helpless father, while their sisters, Antigone and Ismene, selflessly support him and have protected their father in his destitute condition. Oedipus himself praises his daughters for fulfilling the custom of threptra in place of their brothers –

> "... They they could have helped
> my two boys, their father's son-
> then they could have stirred themselves.
> They could. They did not a thing
> For lack of a little word from them
> I was cast out
> to drag away my life in wandering beggary.
> Shelter, devoted care, my daily bread,
> everything within a woman's power to give,
> these I owe to my two daughters here.
> Their brothers sold their father for a throne,
> exchanged him for a sceptre and a realm." (Sophocles 442)

Herodotus here noted the seemingly backward customs of the Egyptians, which features in the Theban palace. He asserted that Egyptian daughters are bound to support their parents, irrespective of their wills; unlike other cultures –

> Just as the Egyptians have a climatic peculiar to themselves, and their river is different in its nature from all other rivers, so, too have they instituted customs and laws contrary for the most part to those of the rest of mankind. Among them, the women buy and sell, the men stay at home and weave; and whereas in weaving all others push the woof upwards, the Egyptians push it downwards... No woman is dedicated to the service of any god or goddess; men are dedicated to all deities male or female. Sons are not compelled against their will to support their parents, but daughters must do so though they be unwilling. (Herodotus 2)

In the Theban royalty, the daughters willingly repay their brothers' threptra. Oedipus himself laments the situation –

> Oh what miserable and perfect copies
> they have to be of the Egyptian ways!
> For there the men sit at home and weave
> while their wives go out to win the daily bread,
> as you do, my daughters
> Just so your brothers, who should be
> the very ones to take this load upon them.
> Instead they sit at home like girls
> and keep the house,
> leaving the two of you to face my troubles
> and make life a little easier for me. (Sophocles 337)

This makes *Oedipus at Colonus* unique as it addresses the father-daughter bond unlike other ancient narratives. Antigone plays the role of a caregiver for her father, sacrificing twenty precious years of her life for him. She acts as a support for Oedipus, being his third leg, upon whom he leans physically for support. Oedipus recounts her selfless sacrifice –

> Antigone, from the time she left her childhood behind
> and came into full strength, has volunteered for grief,
> wandering with me, leading the old misery, hungry,
> feet cut through the bristling woods...
> an eternity - worn down by the drenching rains,
> the scorching suns at noon. Hard labour,
> but you endured it all, never a second thought
> for home, a decent life, so long as your father
> had some care and comfort. (Sophocles 376)

In the words of Dorothy Willner, Antigone has foregone her eligibility for marriage and motherhood by surrendering herself in his care. Oedipus unknowingly binds his daughter to satisfy his needs as a surrogate wife or mother and thus compels the normal boundaries between family members to become blurred.

Threpteria as a concept is used in *Homeric Hymn to Demeter* to denote the reward paid to the nurses of the children by their parents. When Demeter goes to King Celeus to be his son Demophoön's nurse, he promises that "if you could bring him up until he reached the full measure of youth, any one of womankind who should see you would straightway envy you, such gifts would our mother give for his upbringing" (Hesiod and Homer 166). Metaneira, his wife, repeats the notion, asserting, "if you should bring him up until he reach the full measure of youth, any one of woman-kind that sees you will straightway envy you, so great reward would I give for his upbringing." (Hesiod and Homer 221)

The legal and social custom of Gêrotrophia has thus been used and represented in the literary context as the concept of threptra, featuring in several ancient narratives, thus reflecting the moral codes of the Greek society.

Works Cited

Cantarella, Eva. "Fathers and Sons in Rome". *The Classical World*, Spring, 2003, Vol. 96, No. 3 (Spring, 2003), The Johns Hopkins University Press, 2003.

Crotty, K. *The Poetics of Supplication: Homer's Iliad and Odyssey*. Cornell University Press, 1994.

Godley, A. D. trans. *Herodotus*. Harvard University Press, 1920.

Greene, Thomas McLernon. *The Descent from Heaven: A Study in Epic Continuity.* Yale University Press, 1963.

Hesiod and Homer. *Hesiod, The Homeric Hymns and Homerica.* Translated by Hugh G. Evelyn-White, William Heinemann Ltd., 1914.

Homer. a. *The Iliad of Homer.* Translated by Alexander Pope, The Project Gutenberg Ebook, 2006. http://www.gutenberg.org/license. Accessed 27 May. 2022.

——— b. *The Odyssey*. Translated by Robert Fagles, Penguin Classics, 1997.

Kirk, G. S. *The Iliad: A Commentary, II.* Cambridge Univ., 1990.

Nussbaum, Martha C. and Juha Sihvola. Eds. *The Sleep of Reason: Erotic Experience and Sexual Ethics in Ancient Greece and Rome.* University of Chicago Press, 2013.

Pratt, L. "The Parental Ethos of the Iliad". *Constructions of childhood in Ancient Greece and Italy*, Hesperia Supplements 41, 2007.

Sophocles. The *Three Theban Plays*. Translated by Robert Fagles, The Penguin Group, 1982.

V

The Parental Ethos Dealt in English Literature from Pre-Shakespearean Era to Modern Age

There is a mysterious bond between the fields of psychoanalysis and literature. Considering parent-child relationship to be not only fundamental to all human relationships, but also pervasive in human existence, the phenomenon is used by authors of all ages in their literary works. The ancient narratives have always served as a model to the entire Western literary canon.

The ancient narrative of Cupid and Psyche gets mirrored in Spenser's *Faerie Queene* (1590). The allegorical romance symbolises the moral and spiritual journey of any individual Christian, who has to protect himself from innumerable temptations of sins to attend glory and truth ultimately. The epic poem featuring the Guyon, aided by a mysterious visored knight and his squire, who has to escape various traps laid by vanity, flattery, ambition, credulity, challenge, and jealousy, reminds the readers and the scholars of Psyche, who also has to confront several difficulties, set by Venus or Aphrodite, in order to get reunited with her divine husband. In Book II of the epic poem, the angel who rescues Guyon is given a very similar description to that of Cupid by Apuleius. Guyon's journey to the underworld coincides often with the final task given to Psyche by Aphrodite, which also entails a tour to the underworld. In both the cases, they fall into a deadly sleep as soon as they enter the underworld. Lastly, both of them are supernaturally assisted to accomplish their individual tasks. Significantly, the characters are guilty about possessing too much curiosity, which instigates them to probe into the divine mysteries. For Psyche, the pagan Gods seem to be real, whereas in case of Guyon, the divine revelation results due to his own superstitious fear and misconceived faith. Initially, Guyon tends to ignore this heavenly grace but later this conviction saves him. In short, Psyche's apotheosis is seen to be prefiguring in Guyon's immortalization, being united with Christ.

In Renaissance England, the parent-child dynamics was based on the fifth Commandment, asserting to "Honor thy father and mother"

(Douglas et al. 1174), but most importantly stressing on "honor[ing] thy father." (Douglas et al. 1174) Nevertheless, modern times are quite different as contemporary parents keep altering their roles as their children grow up, occasionally being a teacher, a confidant, a friend, and often a disciplinarian.

Early England was typically a patriarchal society and this prompted that "Daughters are perhaps the greatest victims of a patriarchal family and Elizabethan daughters were no exception." (Singh 33) "A woman's status depended upon that of her husband, or if she remained single, upon that of her family." (Masek 141) Women had a much lesser status and were almost sold off to live in another man's household, but a man of that time enjoyed complete control over the family. A man had the right to inherit all the lands and titles and was thus brought up and given education so as to take the position of his father. On the other hand, the daughters were treated as properties of men, who had to abide by their orders. They were only trained in household chores and their only duty was to please the men of the house. Fathers would choose the husbands for their daughters which had nothing to do with love. Marriage in the then society was founded on political power and social climbing. "The family and the sate were inextricably intertwined in the minds of English women and men of the sixteenth and seventeenth centuries'; as a consequence, 'we cannot understand politics (as conventionally defined) without understanding the politics of the family.'" (McBride 1) Fathers were known to marry off their daughters by paying a handsome dowry to acquire more property, titles, and thus raise their social status in return. Altogether there had been a substantial difference between the position of men and women in the English society, especially till the Elizabethan age, though it continued even after for quite a number of years. Literature has been seen to reflect the fervour of the age.

Talking about portrayal of mother-daughter relationship in Shakespeare's works, instances are very rare. "Shakespeare seems hesitant to frame a relationship that is about to be broken because most of the daughters in Shakespeare's works are around marrying age." (Benedict) Rather, "it is more common to find fathers and daughters and mothers and sons, but mothers specifically seem to be missing in very different ways." (Benedict) It has been noticed that some plays do not mention about mother figures, while in many others, mothers appear as ghosts; they give birth, die, and return to life. There are also instances where the playwright mentions about the mother's entrance in the stage direction, but they do not appear physically on stage.

The shifting affections of Shakespearean fathers and daughters have gained a great deal of scholarly attention. During the 1970s and the 1980s, literary critics show more sympathy towards the fathers, considering their struggles with their daughters to be among the expected hurdles of a normal family life. Further study discovers a typical possessiveness in excess of normal parental concern in the father's conduct or a capriciousness, coldness, and disloyalty as the case maybe, unwarranted by the exemplary etiquette of the daughters. Some critics often have found an incestuous desire for the daughters in the fathers' motives, while some others have discerned the father's possessiveness as a love corrupted by the rights and powers conferred on him by the patriarchal society of the contemporary period. In such plays, the daughters occupy the central stage, becoming the focal point of the narrative of the play. Shakespearean daughters like Juliet, Ophelia, and Desdemona submitted themselves to the patriarchal structure of the society by moving to the whims of their fathers, Old Capulet, Polonius, and Brabantio respectively, whether willingly or unwillingly. They fall prey to the patriarchal terms of their fathers and their tragedies are thus examples of indictments of sexist oppression, as they have very little option but to accept their defeat. They somehow reflect the father-daughter equations in the ancient narratives where Zeus, by marrying Persephone to Hades against her will and without the consent of her mother Demeter, attempts to gain control over his daughter's fate, though she always has been taken care and nurtured by her mother alone. He also forcibly marries his other daughter Aphrodite to Hephaestus against her will. He considers the marriage to be the only way to save others from rivalry to win the Goddess of Beauty.

The relationship that Shakespearean fathers share with their sons unlike the daughters is much more peaceful. The father-son bond is seen to occupy the centre stage and become the most important factor behind the character development of the sons. Good sons are to be their fathers' protectors as young Hamlet, who saves his father's honour by taking revenge of his wrongful death. Often sons like Edmund in *King Lear* are found to be saving their fathers from an eminent threat. Early modern ideology regarding masculinity proclaims a son's attitude towards his father to be a major indicator of the type of man he is or the kind of personality he possesses.

The Shakespearean play *The Tempest* explores the father-daughter bond, which can be rarely found in the time period between the Renaissance and the Elizabethan age. Being executed from his own dukedom by his brother Antonio, Prospero, the central father-figure, appears to possess a God-like persona for her daughter Miranda in the uninhabited island in which they have taken shelter. He plays the role of both a father and a mother as her mother has died in her childhood and all his actions are motivated by one desire, i.e., to ensure a secured future for his daughter. "I have done nothing but in care of thee, of thee, my dear." (Shakespeare 1073). Miranda is totally ignorant of the outside world because she has come to this island at a very small age; she herself pronounces her ignorance – "More to know / Did never meddle with my thoughts. / I never even considered that there might be more to know" (Shakespeare 1073). She has no one in her company except her father for the entire span of twelve years she has been residing in the island. He has been the sole protector, nurturer, and providers for her – her entire world. At one point in the play, she feels a sense of obligation to her father and so she laments, "Alack, what trouble. Was I then to you!" (Shakespeare 1075), hearing the story of their treacherous journey to the island twelve years ago. To this, Prospero immediately showers his love with the words –

> Oh, a cherubim
> Thou wast that did preserve me. Thou didst smile
> Infused with a fortitude from heaven,
> When I have decked the sea with drops full salt,
> Under my burthen groaned; which raised in me
> An undergoing stomach to bear up
> Against what should ensue. (Shakespeare 1075)

This clearly depicts their mutual dependence on one another. Moreover, Prospero's magical powers contribute to Miranda's God-like view of him. Miranda's ignorance especially allows Prospero to exert his full authority over her and having full control of her; raising her in his image and in turn demanding respect and obedience from her. "Obey, and be attentive" (Shakespeare 1074), Prospero exclaims almost ordering her to pay attention to his words and rebuking her for being inattentive. Like Zeus pre-deciding Persephone's marriage, Prospero also designs the entire plan for his daughter's marriage along with controlling the speed of the progress of the relationship. Hallet Smith interpreted the whole situation – "The young lovers Ferdinand and Miranda are characterized very economically. Miranda's modesty and innocence are appropriate to the romantic situation in which she is placed-that of never having a young man before … Ferdinand, a pampered prince, gladly undergoes servitude and labor for his love" (Smith 5)

In the play, Prospero has been a father-figure not only to Miranda, but also to the other inhabitants of the island like Ariel and Caliban. Ariel too like Miranda feels obligated towards Prospero as he has rescued him from the captivation of Sycorax. Prospero never forgets to remind him of the previous condition the moment he asks for freedom – "Thou liest, malignant thing! Hast thou forgot / The foul witch Sycorax, who with age and envy / Was grown into a hoop? Hast thou forgot her?" (Shakespeare 1076). It is important to note here that Prospero's relation to his daughter should never be compared to his relationship with Ariel since the latter is much of manipulation and less of co-dependency as in the former case. The readers are also informed that Prospero has attempted to father Caliban by teaching him language but he has broken his trust by dishonouring his daughter.

The play also displays an example of a father-son bond through the characters of the King of Naples, Alonso, and his son, Ferdinand. The world shatters around them upon thinking about each other's death. Alonso especially becomes grief-stricken upon believing his son to have died. He begins to lose interest in all the actions happening around him. All the efforts of Gonzalo to console the bereft father seem fruitless. This proves his deep love for him, which gets more and more pronounced when his unfeigned and unrestrained rejoicing at recovering him seems to have no boundaries. Alonso's character in the play depicts the fact that a villain also has a heart to feel. On the other hand, Ferdinand is shown to be a loving and dutiful son. The supposed death of his father seems to lend a pathetic charm to him. He gets stained with sorrow and grief and starts shedding heavenly tears, weeping continuously over the king's wreck. The reunion with his father at the end of the play makes him spellbound with excess of joy and happiness.

The play *King Lear* in contrast depicts a troublesome parent-child relationship as the primary focus of the story. Daughters in that era generally were found to struggle to negotiate a passage into marriage and adulthood with their father's blessings, while the fathers were seen to struggle to relinquish these young daughters to men of their choice, making them their future husbands. The conflicts between man's law and nature's law is witnessed to be at dispute in the play in which the filial theme seems to occupy the central stage. Lear betrays his most loyal daughter Cordelia, and in turn gets betrayed by the pretentious and nasty older daughters, Goneril and Regan. Similarly, a parallel but smaller plot reveals Gloucester betraying his older legitimate son Edgar and gets further betrayed by his fiendish younger illegitimate son Edmund.

Thus, the two fathers both ignore as well as embrace nature's law at the same time. On the other hand, the two daughters of Lear and the son of Gloucester, by ignoring and abandoning their fathers, in actuality renounce the natural law, and thereby attempt to embrace and endorse the Neo-Darwinist argument for the survival of the fittest, which is again the nature's law. This action seems to resonate Ouranos' betrayal of his children and subsequently him getting betrayed by his son Cronus and also Cronus' betrayal of Olympians and his son Zeus' betrayal of him. The consequences are also not much different; following the nature's law, Goneril and Regan like Ouranos and Cronus get destroyed finally.

Towards the end of the play, King Lear is seen lamenting over the death of his younger daughter Cordelia, which reminds the readers of Priam, grieving his son, Hector's death, in *Iliad*. Unlike the two elder daughters, Goneril and Regan, who have adopted a pretension of maintaining a pretty picture of family love while actually being selfish, shallow, narcissistic, and self-centred, the younger daughter of Lear, Cordelia, is a kind and gentle girl, who feels too shy and modest to publicly announce her affection for her father and this makes room for several misunderstandings in Lear's mind regarding Cordelia. He renounces her as his daughter and decides to divide his kingdom among the two elder daughters which leads him to his tragic end. Cordelia has to depart from her paternal household, devoid of any heritage and her father's blessings. Lear, after disposing off his kingdom to his other two daughters, decides to spend his last days with them, but when he reaches their houses, the hostile and spiteful treatment that he receives from his daughters literally drives him mad. On the other hand, although being disowned and exiled by her father, Cordelia, still retains love for him. She manages to reunite with Lear, who has turned to a half-mad beggar in grief. She as a devoted daughter gathers an army, being the Queen of France, and declares war against her sisters to rescue her father. Unfortunately, her forces get defeated soon and she has been imprisoned and executed along with her father by her enemies. At the sight of Cordelia's dead body, Lear's heart-wrenching words reflect the same grief as witnessed in Priam's wailing for Hector's corpse – "Why should a dog, a horse, a rat, have life, / And thou no breath at all?" (Shakespeare 669)

The overall relationship between a father and his daughters as dealt in the play appears to be quite toxic. As a father, Lear is seen to treat his daughters as objects, whose primary obligation is to adore him and return the favour of being nurtured by him, while he has the right to dispense and withhold love according to his mood and desire. He seems to be shuffling from one daughter to another, seeking for the one who will agree to stroke his male ego the most and thus in the process risks not only both his life and kingdom, but also those of his third daughter Cordelia, who feels it to be a moral obligation to serve her father at any cost. Thus, Lear in the play represents an abysmal parent, who destroys all the positive aspects of a healthy father-daughter dynamics.

Apart from the story of Lear and his three daughters, the play also presents a few father-son relationships. The equation between the two sons of Gloucester, Edmund and Edgar, depicts two different aspects of goodness and evil. Edmund and Edgar's relationship with their old father and their treatment of the father highly impacts the readers' perception of the concept of a good son. The conflict between a father and a son is especially conveyed through Gloucester and his betrayal by his bastard son Edmund, which is more than a simple power struggle. The intertwining plots and scandals begin with Edmund creating a forged letter, supposedly and destructively written by his half-brother Edgar, which contains plans of Gloucester's murder. Edmund successfully surpasses the first betrayal and gathers more courage to reach the epitome of evil by plotting against his father, finding ways to cross him with Regan and Cornwall, thereby attempting to enhance his potential inheritance and power. Hence, in this conflict, which is both caused and initiated by Edmund, Gloucester emerges as a victim to the scandal that Edmund has viciously designed. The life which is sought by his favourite son is finally healed under the protecting care of his loyal son, Edgar, whom he has himself wronged by believing the words of his contriving son. This sub-plot serves as a parallel narrative to Lear's tussle with his daughters. The resembling characters of Lear's ostentatious daughters and Edmund serve the purpose of enhancing the readers' insight of the consequences that result due to the exceeding greed for more power. Through instances of the incredible treasons between parents and offspring, the meaning and truth within the play's key theme of betrayal is pronounced. The play also asserts the natural truth that where instinct plays a dominant role, the man's biological inheritance, i.e., judgement, becomes a poor victim of circumstances. Both the dominant father-figures, Lear and Gloucester, get entrapped by their own father instincts, which lead them to favour the monstrous children and disown the benevolent ones, getting misled by their facade of kindness and gracious appearance and thus get doomed themselves at the end. This further establishes the fact that the principle of evil is active in every household of all degrees, whether legitimate or illegitimate.

The play *Hamlet* presents the readers another loving and dutiful son, who can happily sacrifice his life to avenge his murder. Hamlet and his mother Gertrude share an exceptional parent-child connection, which seems to be quite positive though he never approves of her relationship with Claudius, whom she marries soon after the death of his father. The betrayal of his father by his mother has led Hamlet to develop a dismal opinion towards all women in general – "frailty, thy name is woman" (Shakespeare 296). Although this betrayal of a husband by his wife may seem to have a negative implication on the readers, yet it can be considered positive if viewed with a different point of view; perhaps Gertrude is securing the crown for her son who is nowhere near ready to accept kingship, which she is quite aware of and thus by staying the Queen, she makes provision for him so that he can grow up. Here, she can be observed as playing the role of a protective parent. The mother in her overshadows her role as a wife.

The step-parent's roles in the play are painted and demonstrated as very unhealthy. Claudius is the perpetual evil of the entire family. It is Gertrude's marriage to Claudius, which according to many critics forms a greater reason for Hamlet to kill him than his murder of Old Hamlet. Surprisingly, he never for once thinks of killing his mother, rather he politely requests her to "go not to mine uncle's bed" (Shakespeare 317). Here, one can get a clear echo of the ancient Greek narrative of Orestes, who shows no dilemma in killing his uncle Aegisthus for murdering Agamemnon, his father, and for marrying his mother Clytemnestra subsequently, but he has shown enough signs of procrastination in taking the life of his mother and Electra, her sister, has almost to force her to take up the action by reminding him of his role as a dutiful son of their father.

The ending of the play also reflects the mother-son bond when Gertrude calls out her son's name before dying, warning him with the words – "No, no! the drink, the drink! O my dear Hamlet! / The drink, the drink! I am poisoned" (Shakespeare 331). On the other hand, Hamlet also gets devastated by her death and immediately calls everyone around to find the treachery that has led to this terrible outcome. The Freudian analysis of the rendering of the character of the play signifies that the behaviour and the decisions of the titular character of Hamlet are subconsciously driven by Oedipus complex, which lies behind his possessiveness over his mother.

The father-son dynamics as displayed in the play is quite fascinating. Although there is not much information regarding the bond, the father-son duo has shared before the death of Old Hamlet, the amount of respect

Hamlet has shown for his dead father throughout the play seems quite significant. On one occasion, Hamlet compares his father to 'Hyperion' and he has eventually lost his sanity after the ghost of his dead father conveys him the secret behind his murder. His life almost turns purposeless except avenging Old Hamlet's assassination. While comparing his father with his step-father or uncle, his words display actually the deep love and honour he has for him. He describes his father as "Hyperion's curls; the front of Jove himself; / An eye like Mars, to threaten and command; / A station like the herald Mercury / New lighted on a heaven-kissing hill" (Shakespeare 316) in contrast to "a mildewed ear / Blasting his wholesome brother" (Shakespeare 316), the words he uses for Claudius.

In contrast to the family of Hamlet, the parent-child relationship exhibited by Polonius and his two children is worse and an unhealthy one. Polonius always tries to control or dictate their lives unlike Old Hamlet or Gertrude. The second act of the play begins with Polonius' instruction to Reynaldo to defame his son Laertes in order to gain total control over his life, and in the process, he never thinks twice before sacrificing his son's image. Similarly, he also forces Ophelia to rely on him instead of marrying Hamlet. Nevertheless, the readers can see that Ophelia turns insane after his death and Laertes returns to avenge his murder as a responsible and dedicated son.

Though common readers can find some abnormalities in the parent-child equations in the play, it must be remembered that a parent's controlling and intrusive nature was considered to be quite normal in the typical upper-class families in the Elizabethan and Jacobean era.

Shakespearean tragi-comedy *The Merchant of Venice* comes up with three parent-child pairs – two of which are father-daughters, whereas the third one being a comic father-son pair. Although the play is built upon the struggles between a Christian and a Jew, it also forms a rich tapestry threaded with multiple love and self-sacrifice; hatred and revenge; friendship, marriage, and divided loyalties; and legal, emotional, and financial bonding. The most prominent among them is that of Portia's bond with her father, which is probably the most positive one. It is not that Portia's relationship with her father is perfect, but her father has designed his will before his death in such a manner so as to protect her from fortune hunters in his absence as well as it will ensure that her husband values Portia not only for her money and beauty but also accept her as a person she is, but unfortunately Portia resents her father's method of securing her happiness, considering it to be a dead father's interference in the life of a living daughter. Nevertheless, she obeys him. Undeniably, she feels frustrated and resented and hence vents her anger by insulting the suitors at their back, yet she honours her father's wishes even when she finds the traitors to be tempting enough to use sabotage. Even when it was Bassanio's opportunity to pass through the test, she shows faith in her father's wisdom, exclaiming – "if you do love me you will find me out" (Shakespeare 846). She has an inclination towards Bassanio, yet she clearly lets him know that she cannot exert her will in choosing him; to get her, he has to successfully qualify himself in the test.

The second daughter, who finds mention in the play, Jessica, though presented as a positive and a much agreeable character as compared to her father Shylock, is the least loyal of all other children of the play. She secretly allows a Christian, Lorenzo, to court her, though she knows that Shylock will never approve anyone of the Christian faith to be her husband. She also deceives her father; abandons him; and steals plenty of his valuables, including his dead wife Leah's last gift. She rejects her father as a person along with his way of life and his religion altogether, although some pangs of guilt for her father can be observed from her words – "Alack, what heinous sin is it in me / To be ashamed to be my father's child! / But though I am a daughter to his blood, / I am not to his manners" (Shakespeare 840). The readers still do not find the behaviour of Jessica to be deploring especially when they consider Shylock's treatment of her. Shylock has little affection or kindness for her and refuses to consider her as a person in her own right; rather claims that she is an extension of himself to him, being his flesh and blood – "My own flesh and blood to rebel" (Shakespeare 844). Jessica finds it difficult and suffocating to reside with her father and she laments, "Our house is hell" (Shakespeare 840). Shylock tries to isolate her from the entire world by locking her up, but before her elopement, he is seen to retain his trust on her obedience to him – "Hear you me, Jessica: / Lock up my doors; and when you hear the drum / And the vile squealing of the wry-necked fife, / Clamber not you up to the casements then, / Nor thrust your head into the public street / To gaze upon Christian fools with varnished faces; / ... Let not the sound of shallow fopp'ry enter / My sober house" (Shakespeare 841). He never has time to ponder upon her feelings being too much engrossed in contemplating about his money – "I did dream of moneybags tonight" (Shakespeare 841) and his revenge – "I'll go in hate, to feed upon / The prodigal Christian" (Shakespeare 840-841). The readers are further shocked when on discovering that Jessica has fled with his valuables, he shouts out –

My daughter! O my ducats! O my daughter!
Fled with a Christian! O my Christian ducats!
Justice! The law! My ducats and my daughter!
A sealed bag, two sealed bags of ducats,
Of double ducats, stol'n from me by my daughter!
And jewels—two stones, two rich and precious stones,
Stol'n by my daughter! Justice! Find the girl!
She hath the stones with her, and the ducats! (Shakespeare 843)

They get all the more reproachful and seem to lose all sympathy for him on hearing – "I would my daughter were dead at my foot, and the jewels in her ear! Would she were hearsed at my foot, and the ducats in her coffin!" (Shakespeare 845)

The only father-son pair presented in the play lends a comic purpose to the grave narrative. The bond between Launcelot Gobbo and his father is neither enticing as that of Jessica and her father Shylock, nor as caring as Portia and her father; in fact Launcelot initially displays lack of concern and respect for his father, when he banters, "Well, my conscience ... says very wisely to me, 'My honest friend Launcelot, being an honest man's son'—or rather an honest woman's son, for indeed my father did something smack, something grow to, he had a kind of taste" (Shakespeare 838). He also seems quite cruel to the old and helpless man while jesting about his own death – "Master Launcelot. Talk not of Master Launcelot, father; for the young gentleman, / according to Fates and Destines, and such odd / sayings, the Sisters Three and such branches of leaning, / is indeed, deceased; or, as you / would say / in plain terms, gone to heaven" (Shakespeare 838), without having any consideration for the emotional turbulence, which he will be going through on hearing about his only son's death. On the other hand, Old Gobbo is shown to hardly know his son, neither does he recognise him, nor his voice or personality; the only thing that he is certain about is his social status of being a servant and not a master, yet he is seen to be quite fond of his son and considers him to be the only support for his old age – "The boy was the very staff of my age, my very prop" (Shakespeare 838).

The play not only conveys that parental control is best paired with loving concern but also that a good parent loves, cares, as well as understands his child. An ideal parent-child bond should include a healthy measure of wisdom and understanding along with duty and love towards one another.

In the play *The Two Gentlemen of Verona*, the readers are presented with a rebellious and strong-willed daughter Silvia, who is forced by her disagreeable father to get married to the boorish and wealthy suitor Sir Thurio, though she is in love with Valentine. Like the chief plots in most other Shakespearean comedies, Silvia launches a slow but progressive and intensified rebellion against her father, rather than being prompt and impulsive. Instead of opting for a hasty confrontation with her father, she stays innocent with her insubordination. She even plans to elope with Valentine, especially when her father, the Duke of Milan, banishes Valentine from his dukedom. She decides to run away to the forest, where Valentine has set up his camp and joined a band of thieves. The play ends with her silence being coincidental with the end of her disobedience, and the Duke appears onstage to bestow his blessings on Valentine, thereby accepting him as his daughter's husband. The Duke's decision to give consent to his daughter's marriage of her choice, calls for the reconciliation between a father and a daughter, thus resuming the ethical ideals of feminine behaviour. This stresses on the fact how obedience and silence heavily impact and are central to those ideals, leading finally to a happy ending as per the demand of a comedy. The law of the Father must be established in order to retain peace and harmony. Shakespeare thus necessarily ends his plays, thereby silencing the daughters finally by submission either through marriage or death. The next instance of submission by marriage can be witnessed in his other play, *The Taming of the Shrew*, in which the father-daughter bond is featured to be manipulated in various manners.

The play opens with the older daughter of Baptista Minola, a lord in Padua, Katherina or Kate, being described as excessively disobedient and outspoken. Her notorious assertiveness and wilfulness cause numerous men, including Tranio, to deem her as an unworthy option for marriage. On the other hand, her younger sister Bianca, having a composed and gentle nature, seems to be the choice of many suitors, namely Hortensio and Gremio. Nevertheless, their father Baptista has sworn to get his haughty elder daughter married before his younger docile one. Much similar to the other Shakespearean fathers, Baptista wishes to metaphorically sell his daughter to the highest bidder, thus making himself an equally disagreeable character to the audience.

Petruchio, a fortune seeker from Verona, arrives in Padua, being disguised as Litio, following the words of his friend Hortensio. He presents himself as a submissive gentleman who pretends that Kate's shrewd words seem actually kind and gentle to him. This seemingly agreeable nature of Petruchio finally tricks Katherina to get convinced to marry him. Everything changes after marriage. In Verona, Petruchio adopts several cunning means to tame his new wife, often by refusing to provide her food and clothing. The play finally ends with Katherina emerging to be a loyal, tame, and passive wife, while the apparently meek Bianca ends up being defiant and manipulative and elopes with the suitor of her choice behind her father's back. She even disobeys her husband Lucentio and refuses to submit to his will. However, in spite of the tumultuous familial relationships, order seems to be restored as the play outwardly contributes towards the reunification of the family. The comedy aims to highlight the importance of respect and filial responsibility as an integral part of the domestic order, which seems to uphold the national order and harmony within the state. The Elizabeth and Jacobean society pondered upon the biblical teaching on the subject, which becomes prominent from the assertion in the New Testament –

> Children, obey your parents in the Lord: for this is right. Honour thy father and mother; which is the first commandment with promise; That it may be well with thee, and thou mayest live long on the earth. And, ye fathers, provoke not your children to wrath: but bring them up in the nurture and admonition of the Lord. Servants, be obedient to them that are your masters according to the flesh, with fear and trembling, in singleness of your heart, as unto Christ. (Ephesians)

Marriages in the Shakespearean era were not bonded with love from either side of the partners, rather it was associated with exchange of property from one family to another, and due to this social norm, the dynamic between fathers and daughters had been quite disturbing. The father-daughter pair, Cymbeline and his daughter Innogen, often called Imogen, portrays the story of a tumultuous bond in the play of the same name. The plot of the play has its focal point in the daughter moving out of the periphery of her paternal control and starting to make individual choices, which invites distress in the lives of the characters involved.

The wise, beautiful, and resourceful British princess, the daughter of Cymbeline, Imogen incurs her father's rage when she chooses to marry an orphaned gentleman Posthumus, whom Cymbeline raises from childhood, instead of his stepson Cloten. Cymbeline however banishes Posthumus and the struggle begins, though at the end of the play, Imogen, who has been accused even by her husband of infidelity, has to prove her loyalty to finally get reunited with her husband and father.

The play *Romeo and* Juliet, written by Shakespeare, is yet another comedy, which deals with the father-daughter bond. During the play, Lord Capulet, the patriarch of the family, seems to have a caring and protective attitude towards his daughter Juliet as long as she pays heed to his words and conforms to his decisions. According to him, he can think best for his daughter and hence forces her to marry Paris. Juliet repeatedly tries to put forward her opinion, "Good father, I beseech you on my knees/ Hear me with patience but to speak a word." (Shakespeare 1030) to which he sternly replies, "Hang thee, young baggage, disobedient…" (Shakespeare 1030), though initially, when Paris asks for Juliet's hand, he introduces her as "yet a stranger in the world" (Shakespeare 1011) and informs him that she is not yet fourteen, which is two years away from being prepared to be a bride. Hearing this, when Paris further exerts pressure, saying – "Younger than she are happy mothers made" (Shakespeare 1011), Capulet replies, "And too soon marr'd are those so early made" (Shakespeare 1011). He also asks for a little understanding, saying, "The earth hath swallow'd all my hopes but she, / She is the hopeful lady of my earth" (Shakespeare 1011). Juliet is the only surviving heiress to Capulet and hence only "hopeful lady of [his] earth" (Shakespeare 1011). He allows Paris to woo her, but clearly states that "My will to her consent is but a part" (Shakespeare 1011), which means that he wills to acknowledge her say in the marriage. Unfortunately, as the play progresses, he undergoes a change of heart; his enmity gains more priority rather than his love for her daughter.

Apart from Lord Capulet and his wife Lady Capulet, who has never built a close bond with her daughter and is addressed by her daughter as 'Madam', Juliet has a wet nurse, whom she considers to be her closest guardian. Her nurse has been with her from her very childhood even in absence of her mother and she has always addressed her with loving informal words as 'lamb' and 'ladybird', signifying the doting relationship she shares with her.

Romeo's relationship in the play, on the other hand, is worth giving special attention. In the opening scene, when Benvolio inquiries about Romeo to his parents, seeing him wandering alone in the woods before dawn, Romeo's mother Lady Montague immediately displays her loving motherly concern, asking – "O, where is Romeo? saw you him to-day? / Right glad I am he was not at this fray" (Shakespeare 1010); and his father Lord Montague also gets worried and believes that he should not be left alone. Montague further informs Benvolio that Romeo often strolls in the wood – "Many a morning hath he there been seen, / With tears augmenting the fresh morning dew, / Adding to clouds more clouds with his deep sighs" (Shakespeare 1010). He remains concerned not only with his son's abnormal behaviour of weeping and sighing while loitering aimlessly, but also has observed him to close the shutters when the sunlight comes in so as to stay in the dark. He opines that Romeo needs to be counseled – "Black and portentous must this humor prove, / Unless good counsel may the cause remove" (Shakespeare 1010). He has tried many times to know the reason behind his melancholy, but Romeo neither divulges anything to him nor to others; rather he is unwilling to talk to anyone. Montague compares his son to a flower bud, eaten up by a warm from the inside – "the bud bit with an envious worm, / Ere he can spread his sweet leaves to the air, / Or dedicate his beauty to the sun" (Shakespeare 1010). Both the parents feel relieved knowing that Benvolio, Romeo's cousin, volunteers to counsel him. Unlike the authoritative Lord Capulet, the Montagues were permissive parents and have very little control over him. They get involved only when he gets exiled.

Like Juliet's wet nurse, Friar Lawrence also plays a very important role of a guardian in Romeo's life. To Romeo, he is an advisor, a friend, and at the same time, a guide, for whom Romeo has enough respect. He is the only one who approves Romeo's relationship, seeing it as a means to end the feud between the two rival households. After being banished for killing Tybalt, the Friar bestows unwavering support to Romeo. Friar Lawrence's bond with Romeo as a surrogate father here resembles Phoenix and Patroclus's relationship with Achilles.

Both the main protagonist children of the play, Romeo and Juliet's decisions are highly impacted by the parental figures, which has led the 'star-crossed lovers' to sacrifice their lives as they know that their love does not have the power to put an end to the family rivalry, which has been way stronger than their fondness for one another. The parents have treated their children as objects very similar to the divine parents of Hesiod's *Theogony*, who made every possible attempt to control the lives of their children, thereby ultimately ruining them.

The Shakespearean tragedy *Othello* features a father-daughter conflict, which begins when Desdemona secretly marries Othello, thereby defying the patriarchal world to embrace the love of her life. Brabantio, Desdemona's father, refuses to accept black Othello as his daughter's husband. He complains to the Duke, accusing Othello of deceiving his daughter, but gets completely shocked when Desdemona herself announces that she trusts him completely and has chosen him out of her own accord. Thus, Desdemona challenges the patriarchal Renaissance ideology by making a choice of her own instead of submitting herself to the traditional stereotypical role of a good woman.

The history play *King Henry IV* projects a father, getting agitated by the carefree and charismatic nature of his son, Harry or Hal, who cares least for nobility as well as for the throne and hence, King Henry wills to replace him by Harry Percy, a great leader. Like the fathers of the ancient Greek narratives, Peleus, Priam, Laertes, and others, he wants his son to be a brave warrior like Achilles, Hector, Paris, Troilus, or Odysseus. Nevertheless, King Henry towards the end of the play enjoys some bliss when his son proves himself to be an equally good king and warrior.

Submission to father, which symbolises conformity to authority and tradition, often proves to have an adverse effect in the lives of Shakespearean sons like Romeo, Henry, or Hamlet. The daughters like Cordelia, Juliet, and Desdemona however face disaster in disobeying their fathers, though Cordelia among them emerges diviner than the rest. Hamlet submits himself to the code of his father, thereby willingly accepting blood and revenge, while King Lear, the father, is finally won back by her honest and genuine daughter, with whom he wishes to spend the remainder of his life in bliss, though fate seems to have other plans for him. Most of the tragedies of the Elizabethan playwrights involving the parent-child dynamics end in death and regret, while the comedies end in happiness, reunion, and celebration, thus being true to their definitions.

After Shakespeare, many authors of the West have used the parent-child bond as the primary motif in their works and referred to the Greek narratives to delineate their characters and their roles in the texts. Both the Oedipus complex and the Electra complex have been featured in Eugene O' Neill's *Electra* (1931); the title itself is named after the Greek narrative of Electra. The book is divided into three parts – *Homecoming*, *The Hunted*, and *The Haunted*. The first part begins with the end of the civil war. Lavinia Mannon is very excited as her father Brigadier General Ezra Mannon and her brother Orin Mannon are returning from war. Seth Beckwith, the old housekeeper of the Mannon family, informs Lavinia that her mother Christine is lately seen to spend too much quality time with Captain Adam Brant, a single sea captain, who is perhaps the illegitimate son of Lavinia's long-lost uncle David Mannon, disowned for having an affair with a nursemaid and getting her pregnant. Lavinia tries to confirm her apprehension by confronting Brant and her mother, whom she warns against any adulterous relationship. Christine on one hand falsely promises Lavinia to do so, while on the other hand, she conspires with Brant to murder Ezra by replacing his medicine with poison, which will facilitate Ezra's death to appear as a natural one and they can easily escape from getting caught.

Lavinia seeing his father's return after a week gets elated and shares an intense and passionate moment with him. Ezra, pleased to get reunited with his beautiful wife Christine, conveys his wish to break down the wall between them. They make love and Ezra realises that Christine is not enjoying his company; rather she wants to get away from him. This results into a big quarrel between them. Christine reveals to him about her affair with Brant and manages to make him consume the poison as medicine. The poison soon begins to act, but before Ezra expires, he successfully divulges the truth to Lavinia, which shocks her. She finds the box of poison, being unnoticed by Christine.

As Orin returns from the war, Lavinia warns him against their mother, but he remains thrilled to meet her. Here, the readers witness an oedipal bond especially when the mother and son embrace each other. When Orin inquires about Brant, she lies to him that Brant is courting Lavinia. This makes Orin suspicious about Lavinia, though he agrees to keep an eye on Christine and Brant.

The night after Ezra's funeral when Brant has been walking aboard the deck of his ship, Christine informs him that Lavinia has already discovered the truth of the murder, and hence they must escape to China. This entire conversation gets secretly overheard by Lavinia and Orin. Infuriated, Orin shoots Brant and gives it an appearance of a robbery. Hearing of Brant's death, Christine commits suicide by shooting herself. Lavinia considers this action to be divine justice, but Orin feels guilty, and this tortures his peace of mind.

The narrative takes a leap of one year and Orin and Lavinia returns from China. Both of their appearances have undergone a drastic transformation; Orin looks haggard as he cannot leave the past behind, while Lavinia resembles her mother in beauty and sensuousness, which mesmerizes her neighbour Peter. Lavinia agrees to marry Peter and live a happy life with him but Orin's condition worries her. A month later, Orin tells Lavinia that he has written a manuscript, detailing the crimes of the Mannon family, in which a considerable portion is about her. This makes her furious and Orin accuses her of getting sexually attracted to a native Avahanni, which she readily accepts, but on hearing this, Orin instantly attacks her. He also hands over the manuscript to Hazel, Peter's sister, with whom he has been in a love relationship for long. He insists that she should give her brother the manuscript to read if she sees him getting close with Lavinia. Hegel lets him know that she can do anything for him if he surrenders to her, but Orion clearly lets her know that it is all over between them and forces her to leave him alone.

Orin next turns to Lavinia and puts forward a strange demand. He desires to have a sexual relationship with her, which infuriates Lavinia as she wishes him to be dead. Orin immediately starts believing that this would be just. He goes into his study, informing Peter, who has just returned, that he is going to clean his pistol, but there he shoots himself dead. The novel ends with Lavinia undergoing a tragic transformation. She appears to be dull, dark, and grim like her old self. She grows insane and addresses Peter as Adam, clinging unnaturally to him. Peter too gets suspicious of her behaviour. Even Hazel accuses her for making her brother crueller. At last, she decides to isolate herself from everyone and shuts herself behind the door, being among the Mannon ancestors, waiting for her own doom.

The play mirrors Aeschylus's trilogy, which includes *Agamemnon*, *The Libation Bearers*, and *The Eumenides*, where the town people play the role of the Greek chorus. Neill himself justifies the title – "By the title Mourning Becomes Electra I sought to convey that mourning befits Electra; it becomes Electra to mourn; it is her fate; black is becoming to her and it is the color that becomes her destiny." (Kellman)

Henrik Ibsen, a Victorian playwright, wrote a play called *Peer Gynt*, which clearly demonstrates the presence of Oedipus complex in the main protagonist of the play. The five-act verse play, first published in 1867 and then produced in 1876 in Norway, features a rogue, whose character is based upon a legendary Norwegian folk hero, who seems to get destroyed, being finally rescued by the love of a woman.

Peer Gynt is described as a charming but lazy and arrogant peasant boy, who leaves his home to find his fortune. Though he remains confident of his success, he meets with quite a number of disastrous adventures one after the other. He attends a wedding party of a wealthy young woman, where he meets with a young lady named Solveig, who instantly falls in love with him, but Peer impulsively elopes with the bride from the wedding and thereafter abandons her subsequently. Next, he makes several fantastic voyages around the world in which he finds fame and wealth, but remains devoid of happiness. After spending years of uncertainty, he returns to Norway, where his true love Solveig has been waiting for him all through these years. Finally, the play ends with old and disillusioned Peer, getting redeemed by the love of the dedicated and loyal Solveig.

In the play, Ibsen demonstrates a peculiar relationship between Peer and his mother Aase. Even after Peer grows up, their conversation is more like a young mother interacting with her little boy. According to Groddeck, "There can be no two opinions about it; for Aase, Peer is always the little boy whose behaviour he shows us, and for Peer, Aase is the never-ageing mother, the beloved playmate. They live together in a play-world, and for neither of them is there any reality outside. In their world no one else has, nor ever will have, any share." (Groddeck 64) Even after Aase's death, Peer finds a new mother in Solveig, whom he sees as the reincarnation of Aase. On the other hand, very similar to Aase, Solveig considers Peer from the very first meeting to be a king among men, who can ride through air, which makes her more of a mother-substitute. Peer tries to escape from the ties of the mother-fixation on various occasions by getting involved with other women; for the first time with Ingrid, the bride, whom he has stolen from the wedding party; next with the three milkmaids; and finally with the princess of the Troll Mountain. Groddeck briefs the life of Peer as, "Out of the mother we come at birth, back to the mother we must go at death – in and out and roundabout. Narrow is the path at birth, narrow the way to the grave. Birth, the grave, and always the mother. Women stand at the back of us, mother, bride and wife". (Groddeck 79)

Henrik Ibsen uses the theme of Electra complex or, in Freudian term, 'Negative Oedipus Complex' or 'Feminine Oedipus Attitude', in yet another play *Rosmersholm*, published in 1886 and performed in 1887. The plot of the play revolves around an ex-parson named Johannes Rosmer, a representative of high ethical standards, and the adventurous Rebecca West. Both these characters are seen to be in love with each other, though they get haunted by Rosmer's dead wife Beata, who has committed suicide under the subtle provocation of Rebecca West and due to her husband's high-minded indifference in having a sexual relationship with her. Later, Rebecca rejects Rosmer's proposal, stating her guilt of driving Beata to commit suicide in order to take Rosmer under her control. Soon, both Rebecca and Rosmer, distraught with guilt and grief, can neither trust one another nor any other person around them. Rebecca also feels guilty of having an incestuous relationship with her adoptive father Dr. West at one point of time, whom she later suspects to be her biological father in reality. Nonetheless, upon realising that Rebecca and Rosmer can no longer continue the relationship with each other, Rosmer instructs Rebecca to prove her devotion to him by jumping into the mill-race in the same way in which Beata killed herself, to which Rebecca willingly agrees. She also in turn pleads Rosmer to remove her corpse from the water after her death, but instead he decides to die together as they cannot live together.

Sigmund Freud provides a psychoanalytic analysis to the fate of Rebecca – "everything that happened to her [Rebecca] at Rosmersholm, her falling in love with Rosmer and her hostility to his wife, was from the first a consequence of the Oedipus Complex, an inevitable replica of her own relations with her mother and Dr. West". (Freud, 330) Rebecca's rejection of Rosmer's marriage proposal, according to Freud, is prompted by her guilt of developing an incestuous relationship to Dr. West. The feminist critic Toril Moi opines in this regard that probably life has changed so vigorously for Rebecca that it took away the sexual desire from her.

The next but most eminent text dealing with the Oedipus complex is *Sons and Lovers* (1913) by D. H. Lawrence. The semi-autobiographical novel forms a psychological study of the familial and love relationships that the members of an English working-class family are engaged in. The novel begins with introducing Gertrude Morel, an intelligent middle-class woman, who leads an unhappy married life with a coal miner of the town of Westwood named Walter Morel. She finds her solace in her eldest son William, and remains engrossed in him, while her second son Paul grows up and works in a factory, taking up painting as his hobby. He has been almost ignored by her in his initial years, until William dies of a skin disease. Plunged into grief, Gertrude now turns her entire attention to Paul, who revives her with love and care, and with time, the two gets inseparable from each other.

As a young man, Paul gets attracted to a chaste and religious girl, Miriam Liver, who lives in a nearby farm and their initial platonic relationship soon turns into an intense and romantic one, though they never get physically intimate with each other. Mrs. Morel does not accept this happily as she feels that perhaps Miriam is trying to separate her son from her. She grows more and more insecure with time. Meanwhile, Paul shifts his attention from the pious Miriam to an older and sensual woman, Clara Dawes, who stays separated from her husband, Baxter Dawes. Nevertheless, Paul and Miriam share an intimate moment with each other, which makes Paul lose interest in her, upon realising that he does not want to be bound to her either by love or by marriage.

A romance starts blossoming between Paul and Clara and as a result he gets into a savage fight with her estranged husband one night. Elsewhere, Mrs. Morel develops a tumour and suffers vigorously. It becomes impossible for Paul to bear her pain and one day he overdoses her with morphia. Paul surprisingly reunites Clara and Baxter, whom he has befriended since their brawl. Paul in absence of his mother loses all the charm of life, and with Mr. Morel, shifts to a different locality. He feels lost and even loses the zeal to paint any more. At this point of time, Miriam returns to make a final appeal to him to renew their relationship, but he again rejects her. Towards the end of the novel, he feels dejected and even decides to commit suicide one night, but a sudden transformation takes place; he changes his mind and resolves never to submit to the darkness, which keeps tempting him. Thus, the novel ends on a positive note.

The plot of the novel displays several glimpses of the presence of Oedipus complex as an important motif incorporated in the text. Gertrude Morel finds her husband's habits of drinking, squandering the earnings, loitering with friends, dominating her, and throwing her out of the house on a chilly night during pregnancy to be intolerable and he considers him to be incompetent. This also nurtures in her children, especially in William and Paul, a repressed desire to eliminate their father, while at the same time they all harbour an unnatural attraction for their mother. William is seen in the first chapter to enjoy the wakes only in the presence of his mother and feels dejected once she leaves him. He also shares his egg-cups with his mother only, which he has won in a competition. Mr. Morel whereas is left in the house only as a bread winner.

Paul, the second son, is born weak and effeminate, being brought in the world in a dire state. Gertrude promises to love him with 'all her soul' (Joyce 45) once he is born. When Paul suffers from pneumonia, he always longs to stay with his mother. He also draws inspiration from her in his painting and suffers from great distress and discomfort, being distanced from her. After William's death, often the mother and son duo spend little moments of romantic escapades, having adventures together; going about the town, shopping, dining at restaurants, and visiting different places with the excitement of lovers. When Mr. Morel meets with an accident and ends up getting hospitalised, Paul emerges to be the man of the house.

Gertrude can never bear the presence of any other woman in the lives of his sons. She has been jealous of Lily, William's fiancé, as well as the girls, who would send him romantic letters. She considers them as her competitors. William till his death suffers pitiably getting torn between his mother and his lover. Later, when Paul gets engaged to Miriam, Gertrude suffers from the same kind of insecurity. Paul too ultimately resents Miriam as his mother suffers due to her. Paul considers Clara to be a mother-substitute and perhaps so gets involved with her. He beats Baxter, a father-figure for her, though later he reconciles with him, which can be interpreted as his guilt of attempting to get rid of his father-figure.

Earlier, Paul once desires to stop his mother from sleeping next to Mr. Morel, which reminds the readers and the critics of Hamlet's efforts to debar his mother from sharing his uncle and step-father Claudius's corrupt and sinful bedsheets.

When Gertrude dies, Paul visits her body and his near necrophilic act of kissing and stroking the corpse reveals his pent-up desires. He starts seeking someone like his mother in her absence, who claims him strongly with a smoothing, jealous, and destructive love, and hence he again refuses to get involved into a sacrificial marriage with Miriam, when she returns to him. Lawrence describes his future without his mother as an artificial feel of freedom and hope in the image of the city's 'gold phosphorescence' (Joyce 446).

The novel of George Eliot, *Silas Marner* (1861), recounts the story of a weaver of Raveloe, which can be thematically linked with the tale of Demeter and Persephone. The novel begins with Silas, the weaver, being wrongly accused of stealing the congregation's fund. His friend William Dane has framed the whole incident to marry Silas's betrothed. Seeing that God has not helped him to prove himself innocent, he turns into an atheist and flies from Latern Yard to Raveloe in Warwickshire and leads an isolated life. In Warwickshire, the younger son of the landowner Squire Cass, Dunsey Cass, steals Silas's last asset, his two bags of gold and escapes. Godfrey Cass, the elder son of the Squire, on the other hand, marries Molly Farren secretly and she gives birth to his daughter. When Molly attempts to come to reveal Godfrey's truth about their child to everyone, unfortunately she dies on the way and Silas rescues the little girl named Eppie and begets her as his own daughter. Elsewhere Godfrey again marries Nancy. Silas believes that his lost gold has returned to him in the form of the golden-haired child, which gives him immense joy and satisfaction. Both Godfrey and Dolly Winthrop, a neighbour, financially supports Silas to bring Eppie up. Sixteen years pass and Godfrey and Nancy remain childless. Godfrey now comes to claim Eppie back, but this time Eppie refuses. Meanwhile, Dunsey's skeleton gets discovered at the bottom of the stone quarry, which is not far from Silas's home, and with him, the gold bags also lay there. The novel ends with Eppie marrying Aaron, the son of Dolly.

In the narrative, Silas loses his most prized possession, his bags of gold, to the underground, very similar to Demeter, who has lost her prized possession, her daughter Persephone, to the God and King of the underworld, Hades. Silas like Demeter feels completely lost on losing his valuables, and like Demeter, feels complete only by recovering his losses, though in this case, by getting a golden-haired daughter, whom he considers to be the substitute of his gold.

In 1868, William Morris writes an epic poem, *The Earthly Paradise*, retelling various Greek and Scandinavian myths and legends. The plot features a company of Norsemen seeking an Earthly Paradise, where none grows old, which is considered to be analogous to Hesiod's description of the Golden age in *Works and Days*. They finally reach an anonymous city, where the Greek Gods are still worshipped. Very similar to the ancient Greek convention, a feast is organised twice every month, where one tale is told by one of the elders in the city while the other one by one of the wanderers. The classical subjects having the Norse and other medieval sources are most frequently recounted on these occasions.

The Greek myth of the Daedalus-Icarus lends a basic structure of James Joyce's most accessible novel, *A Portrait of the Artist as a Young Man* (1916). The work unites the central themes of individual rebellion and self-discovery and traces the path of development of an artist's individual philosophy. The name of the protagonist of the novel is purposefully chosen, having a link with the ancient mythical Greek hero Daedalus, who with his son Icarus gets trapped in a maze. Stephen, like most young fellows of the time, similarly feels himself entrapped in a convoluted maze, featuring dead ends and circular reasoning, in the words of Francis Hackett in his article "Green Sickness".

The plot of the bildungsroman novel narrates the first formative years of Stephen, detailing the various experiences of his surroundings; his view on faith, family, and country; and demonstrates how these perceptions get into conflict with those the society prescribes for him. This makes him get distanced from the world, but his detachment is misconstrued by the people around to be the arrogance of an egoist. Stephen on the other hand can increasingly feel the pain of social alienation, getting isolated from the surrounding.

The novel opens with Stephen's father recounting a tale, which is inspired explicitly from the Daedalus myth –

> Once upon a time and a very good time it was there was a moocow coming down along the road and this moocow coming down along the road met a nicens little boy named baby tuckoo … (Joyce 20)

The stereotypical fairy tale beginning of the novel is a deliberate attempt of the novelist to trigger the general mind-set of a fantasy world. Next the word 'met' is a personification of a bull, which corresponds to the idea of a humanised bull like the Minotaur in the myth.

Daedalus being a consummate craftsman or artificer himself, according to Joseph Campbell, represents the artist-scientist who seems, "curiously disinterested, almost diabolic human phenomenon, beyond the normal bounds of social judgment, dedicated to the morals not of his time but of his art. He is the hero of the way of thought-singlehearted, courageous, and full of faith that the truth, as he finds it, shall make us free". (Campbell 18) Here, one can easily get a glimpse of Stephen's character. Like Daedalus, Stephen creates a world of his own, which has very little pace for the life theories, where the morality appears to be relative and art and science gain more priority than society and its norms.

The imagery of labyrinth is allegorical to the three institutions – the church, the family, and the nation, to which Stephen feels psychologically snared until he successfully seeks the key to freedom. Time and again life presents before him a number of riddles, especially when he feels drawn towards mortal sinning again and again, which includes visiting prostitutes, committing sins like masturbation, gluttony, etc.; though each time he multiplies his guilt and self-punishment. He also has to confront the authoritative Minotaurs of his life often in the form of his father's resistance during his trip to Cork; next in chapter five, his friend Davin's persuasion to get involved in his Irish nation and heritage; and lastly, the director of his school's coercion to become a Jesuit. Nevertheless, Stephen like his namesake triumphantly fights all the constraints of the labyrinths of his life that hold him hostage and set himself free from them. Following Aquinas's words, "ad pulcritudinem tria requiruntur integritas, consonantia, claritas" translated as "Three things are needed for beauty, wholeness, harmony, and radiance" (Aquinas), Stephen thus successfully transfers the responsibility of judgement from the society to the hand of an individual. He considers the three terms, wholeness, harmony, and radiance to be relative, i.e., the relevance of the three words in one's life changes from person to person and so if the three institutions – family, church, and nation – cannot stay in harmony with an individual, he or she has no responsibility towards them.

A later work of Joyce, *Ulysses* (1922), considered to be a sequel of *The Portrait of the Artist as a Young Man*, has an intricate link with the Homeric myth of Odysseus. In the novel, Joyce attempts to draw an analogy between early 20th Century Dublin life and the mythic episodes of the ancient epic of Homer, *The Odyssey*. In this regard, Eliot comments, "Joyce manipulates a continuous parallel between contemporaneity and antiquity ... In Ulysses, Joyce used ancient myth as a way of controlling, of ordering, of giving a shape and a significance to the immense panorama of futility and anarchy which is contemporary history." (Eliot) The novel recounts the tale of a single day, 16th June 1904, the day known by the name of Bloomsday. The feelings, thoughts, imaginations, and fantasies of the three chief characters of the novel, Stephen Dedalus, Leopold Bloom, and Molly Bloom, are squeezed into the narrative, which bears a striking relevance to the entire Homeric legend.

The modern journey is described without the characters, Stephen, Leopold Bloom, Molly, Haines, and Mulligan, existing at the backdrop; rather they are shaped in the moulds of the mythical personae. Leopold Bloom, the protagonist, is in deep anguish, being exiled in Dublin, his own homeland. The untimely death of his infant has shattered him completely and made him feel ostracized and isolated. At the same time, he feels humiliated upon suspecting his wife Molly's infidelity. He sets on a voyage to seek an assertive life. Instead of evoking a mythical parallel, Joyce treats Bloom's journey as a modern Odysseus being shipwrecked in his own conjugal life to give the dramatic sequence a mythical dimension. In the ancient classic, Penelope has been surrounded by suitors during Odysseus' ten years of exile, which makes the two characters of two very different time periods and their sufferings seem analogous to each other.

The character of Stephen Dedalus is presented as modern Telemachus. Stephen's own father fails to recognise his artistic aspiration, which makes him disillusioned and enables him to deviate from his creative pursuits. Telemachus in the Homeric narrative has left his motherland Ithaca in search of his father to get guided to protect his country from the hostile suitors of his mother, whereas here Stephen abandons his biological father to find a father-figure in Leopold Bloom to get some inspiration in his artistic ambition. Similarly, Leopold Bloom tries to seek his dead son in Stephen.

The character of Molly emerges as modern Penelope being courted by Blazes Boylan, though unlike Penelope, Molly willingly gets involved into the affair herself. Leopard Bloom's surveillance towards his wife reduces his status to be feminine, while Molly plays the role of a discriminating masculine counterpart.

In the novel, James Joyce never intends to use myth as a device to narrate the plot; instead, he treats the characters as the modern equivalent of the mythical Homeric figures.

Apart from using the ancient Greek myths and narratives as frequent allusions in various literary works of all genres, few are retold as well as translated by the authors of the West, retaining their original plots. John Keats gives a tribute to the Greek goddess Psyche in "Odes to Psyche"

(1819). In the poem, the narrator imagines that he has either dreamt of or come across Psyche, the winged goddess, sleeping in the arms of Eros (Cupid), while wandering in the forest. The narrator gets overwhelmed by the pure and innocent beauty of the deity and immediately vows to build a temple for her, but not from stone; rather by his imagination. The Victorian poet Alfred Lord Tennyson's "Ulysses" (1842), a dramatic monologue written in blank verse, recounts in the voice of the titular hero Odysseus or Ulysses in Latin, his yearning to reclaim his long-lost glory in a final adventure over the seas. In the poem, there is a clear depiction of a father's relentless trust on his prudent son as mentioned in the original Greek epic of Homer, *The Odyssey.*

Greek mythology has left an invaluable heritage of tales to be explored in future. Modern literary geniuses have always considered it to be a privilege to borrow and adapt mythic elements in order to make a contribution to the development of the Western civilization and culture.

Works Cited

Aquinas. qtd. in Anon. "Three things are needed for beauty", https://visualsyntax.net/2021/07/24/three-things-are-needed-for-beauty/. Accessed 1 Jul. 2022.

Benedict, Jillian. "Mother-Daughter Relationships in Shakespeare." https://widenerenglish.wordpress.com/2012/10/01/mother-daughter-relationships-in-shakespeare/amp/. Accessed 28 June. 2022.

Campbell, Joseph. "Myth and Dream." *The Hero with a Thousand Faces.* 3rd ed., New World Library, 2008.

Douglas, J. D., et al. "Ten Commandments," *New Bible Dictionary*, Second Edition, Tyndale House, 1982.

Eliot, qtd. in Heffernan, James A. W. *James Joyce's Ulysses: Remixing The Homeric Myth.* https://www.wondriumdaily.com/james-joyces-ulysses/. Accessed 10 Jul. 2022.

Ephesians. qtd. in Anon. "Family Relationships and Filial Duty." https://crossref-it.info/textguide/the-taming-of-the-shrew/43/3387. Accessed 29 June. 2022.

Freud, Sigmund. "Some Character Types met within Psycho – Analytic Work." *On the History of Psycho-Analytic Movement.* The Hogarth Press, 1916.

Groddeck, Georg. "Peer Gynt." *Ibsen: A Collection of Critical Essays*, edited by Rolf Fjelde, Prentice Hall, 1995.

Joyce, James. *A Portrait of the Artist as a Young Man*, edited by. R.B. Kershner, Bedford St. Martins, 2006.

Lawrence, D. H. *Sons and Lovers.* A.I.T.B.S. Publishers, 2009.

Masek, Rosemary. *Women of England: From Anglo-Saxon Times to the Present.* Archon Books, 1979.

McBride, Kari B. *Domestic Arrangements in Early Modern England*. Duquesnes UP, 2002.

"Mourning Becomes Electra – Summary." Edited by Steven G. Kellman, eNotes.com, Inc., 2006. https://www.enotes.com/topics/mourning-becomes#summary-summary-summary-the-work. Accessed 10 Jul. 2022.

Shakespeare, William. *The Arden Shakespeare: Complete Works*. Edited by Richard Proudfoot, et al. Methuen Drama, 2001.

Singh, Sarup. *Family Relationships in Shakespeare and The Restoration Comedy of Manners*. Oxford UP, 1983.

Twentieth Century Interpretations of The Tempest. Edited by Hallett Smith, Prentice-Hall, 1969.

VI

Conclusion: An Evolutionary Critique of the Socio-Grammatical Studies of Diversified Parent–Child Relationships

The term parent-child relationship denotes a unique and enduring bond that exists between a caregiver and his or her child. However, early Greeks and Romans have stuffed their mythologies with tales about Gods and Goddesses, heroes and warriors, the creation of the world, and the family relationships that existed in that era, which may often present narratives that are quite unexpected in the present context. Myths are known to have sprung before the advent of religion, and religious narratives are retellings of those universal mythical themes. Besides religion, society and culture also have been highly influenced by the series of myths of ancient Greeks and Romans.

To define 'culture', it is important to understand the various connotations attached or related to the word. Culture literally means the way of life of an individual, which also includes his or her beliefs, customs, objectives, language, and also the institutions, he or she adheres to and the techniques, he or she adopts to fit himself or herself in the community. Precisely, it permeates every aspect of human life and determines the individual's behaviour predominantly, including the linguistic behaviour. Language on the other hand essentially affects human thinking as well as the individual's way of viewing the world around. The Greek mythology has a profound influence upon the Western society and culture from the pre-Christian era till the modern times. The cultural historian Jacques Barzun commented in this regard, "What links myth with literature ... the imagination." (Marie Fernandes)

The phrase 'parent-child relationship' incorporates and comprehends all possible facets of interconnectivity that characterizes the entire human reproductive mechanism and unit, involving men, women, and their offspring. It is to be noted that here the word 'offspring' encompasses the progeny of all ages and not only youngsters. The various parent-child bonds exemplified and described in the dissertation have different functional, affective, psychological, and institutional aspects. The functional commitments of providing love, care, nurture, and shelter, which are typical to the bond and which often are seen to undergo a reversal of beneficiaries over the course of life, are considered to be less strenuous and wearisome by the affective dynamics that laid the foundation of all such relationships.

The Greek philosopher Aristotle is known to have written two notable ethical treaties – first, the *Nicomachean Ethics*, which states that the contemplative life circumscribes the participation of human soul in the eternal, which can be achieved through a communion of the rational faculty of the soul and the 'nous' (mind or intellect), imparting intelligibility to the cosmos; and the second, being the *Eudemian Ethics*, which pronounces the various factors that make human life worth living. These two are written on the pretext that man should aim to achieve an excellent virtuous character as a precondition for obtaining happiness or well-being (*eudaimonia*) in life. Happiness to Aristotle is an activity of the soul, which depends on a person's actions rather than on his fate. He further emphasizes that ethics must be implemented in practical life rather than being theorised. In the *Nicomachean Ethics*, Aristotle asserted that various virtues like justice, friendship, etc. must be incorporated in human life from the very childhood; the training of which is quite a lengthy process and begins in the '*oikos*' (household). The parents in this case directly play the important role of the contributors, whose nurturing and disciplining activities will help to bring about something new and ordered, i.e., virtuous, out of '*akolasia*' (wildness).

According to Aristotle, the parents are ethically adequate owing to their early training and experiences of life, and hence their actions will serve as the primary source of the ethical '*telos*' (virtue) for the child. Once, the child grows up, his or her '*telos*' will be marked both by freedom from the ethical guidance of the caregivers, being competent to fend for himself or herself, and through resemblance to the parents in their virtual disposition.

The affinity that progenitors and their progeny feel towards one another is a very natural emotion that human world shares with the animal world. The Book VIII of the *Nicomachean Ethics* deals with the theme of different kinds of friendship among relatives, which are said to be actually derived from the affection of parents for their offspring. Parents, in the words of Aristotle, consider their children to be part or rather extension of themselves, while the children love their parents, acknowledging them to be the source of their being. Here, he also emphasizes that the love or friendship that the parents and the children feel for one another is not equal from both sides as generally progenitors are more attached to their progeny than the reverse, since the longing that a source feels for its parts is much more than what the part feels for its source. Another important reason behind it is that the parents start loving their children the moment they are born to them but the children discern affection for their parents only once they develop the faculty of understanding, so time is truly a dominating factor. This fact also explains why mothers feel the parental affection more in them than the fathers. Children on the other hand love their parents just like men love God, who is superior to them. Parents act as a substitute to God in their lives as they are the ones who bestow on them the greatest benefits, giving them their lives, food, shelter, and then education. Hence, the friendship between the parents and the children is both of pleasure and utility.

In the modern age, with regard to the psychological aspect, the emergence of modern science of psychology has demonstrated an increase in the awareness of the influence that parents have on the behavioural patterns of children and their personality development.

The parent-child dynamics can be defined in terms of its structure using the structural model, which lends a framework for the examination of the triadic bond, consisting of father-mother-child. This triadic model involves the operation of four dual-directional dyadic interpersonal relationships – father-son, father-daughter, mother-daughter, and mother-son. This dyadic structure in the relationships definitely begins as biological reality in the initial phase, but the forms and extent of their perpetuation differ considerably in the practical life. The family in which the individual participates as a child from birth is described as his or her natal family, whereas the conjugal family, where he or she participates as a parent, is his or her family of procreation. Aristotle described the latter as a natural instinct, in which a man and a woman is involved not only for mere procreation, but also for utility and pleasure, very similar to that of between parents and children.

> ... the friendship between parents and children will be enduring and equitable, when the children render to the parents the services due to the authors of one's being, and the parents to the children those due to one's offspring. (Aristotle 477)

It cannot be denied that the children play a very important role in the lives of their parents. Children are very important for a successful marriage as they emerge as a common property that holds a man and a woman together, and hence childless marriages get easily dissolved, having nothing to bind them together.

There has always been a confusion regarding the socio-cultural background of the Greek epics. In view of the nature and genesis of the ancient literature, it has always been debated whether the social context is a poetic fiction, denoting an artificial amalgam or a blend of different historical periods, or if in reality it is set in a society, which existed in the era in which it has been written. The readers and the scholars always get a hint of the Mycenaean world or the latter half of the eighth century BC in the compositions. Moses Finley in *The World of Odysseus*, supporting the historical option in this regard, comments that there is too much of logicality in the depiction of the society to permit its dismissal as a poetic fiction or amalgam, while in *The Use and Abuse of Homer*, I. Morris argues in support of the social background, being set in the contemporary period, which according to him is done purposefully as an attempt to maintain the 'epic distance'. In *A New Companion to Homer*, K. A. Raaflaub felt the necessity to archaize by hinting towards a non-contemporary instead of contemporary social background, "modern enough to be understandable, but archaic enough to be believable" (Raaflaub 624), and hence he designates the place of the depicted society to be in a time frame somewhere in between the late ninth and the eighth century BC.

Apart from the relevance of the social background which forms the setting of the ancient narrative, oikos as a social institution plays a very important role in the functioning of the parent-child dynamics in the narrative. Walter Donlan described the term 'oikos' as "the basic kinship, residential, and economic unit, comprising both 'house' and household" (Donlan). This household comprises of all the human members of the unit, including the master of the house called 'kurios' and the retainers called 'doulos'. Murray while describing minutely the structural framework of the household makes a distinction between the family of the master and the economic section of the household, which includes the servants and their families. Both the two sections are made to "fall under the same semantic umbrella of 'family'" (Patterson 2) by Patterson, but it is only the first one which contributes an area of operation to the development of the parent-child bond.

The entire family structure which existed in the age of Homer, Hesiod, and other ancient Greek literati have undergone a major transformation over years, yet the emotions that lay beneath the relationships between parents and children in those times somewhere remains the same even today. This facilitates the modern authors to draw inspiration from the Greek legendary works.

Works Cited

Aristotle. *Nicomachean Ethics.* Translated by H Rackham, Harvard University Press, 1934.

Donlan, W. "The Social Groups of Dark Age Greece." *Classical Philology.* Vol. 80, No. 4 (Oct., 1985). https://www.jstor.org › stable. Accessed 1 Jul. 2022.

Fernandes, Marie. "Myth and Cult in Literature." https://standrewscollege.ac.in/wp-content/uploads/2018/06/Myth-and-Cult-in-Literature.pdf. Accessed 1 Jul. 2022.

Patterson, C. B. *The Family in Greek History.* Harvard University Press, 1998.

Raaflaub, K. A. "Homeric Society." *A New Companion to Homer*. Edited by I. Morris & B. Powell, Brill, 1997.

Select Bibliography

Adlington, W. Trans. *Apuleius the Golden Ass being the Metamorphoses of Lucius Apuleius.* W. William Heinemann ltd. and G. P. Putnam's sons, 1915.

Aeschylus. *The Oresteia: Agamemnon, The Libation Bearers, The Eumenides*. Translated by Robert Fagles, Penguin Classics, 1977.

———. *Agamemnon.* Translated by Timothy Chappell. https://www.gutenberg.org/files/14417/14417-h/14417-h.htm. Accessed 22 May. 2022.

———. *Eumenides (The kindly ones)*. Translated by Timothy Chappell, https://www.ancient-literature.com/greece_aeschylus_eumenides.html. Accessed 22 May. 2022.

Anon. *The Thebaid.* qtd. in https://www.newworldencyclopedia.org/entry/oedipus. Accessed 18 May. 2022.

Apuleius. qtd. in Anon. "Eros and Psyche," https://www.greeka.com/greece-myths/eros-psyche/. Accessed 12 Jul. 2022.

Aquinas. qtd. in Anon. "Three things are needed for beauty", https://visualsyntax.net/2021/07/24/three-things-are-needed-for-beauty/. Accessed 1 Jul. 2022.

Aristotle. *Nicomachean Ethics.* Translated by H Rackham, Harvard University Press, 1934.

Artemidorus. *The Interpretation of Dreams (Oneirocritica)*. Translated and Edited by Robert J. White, 2nd ed., Original Books, 1990.

Arthur, Marylin. "Politics and Pomegranates: an Interpretation of the Homeric Hymn to Demeter". *The Homeric Hymn to Demeter: Translation, Commentary, and Interpretive Essays*. Edited by Helene P. Foley, Princeton University Press, 2013. https://doi.org/10.1515/9781400849086-024. Accessed 25 May. 2022.

Avery, Harry C. "Achilles' Third Father". Franz Steiner Verlag, 1998. https://www.jstor.org/stable/4477270. Accessed 2 Jan. 2022.

Barchilón, Jacques. "Beauty and the Beast: From Myth to Fairy Tale." *Psychoanalysis and the Psychoanalytic Review* , 46 (1959).

Benedict, Jillian. "Mother-Daughter Relationships in Shakespeare." https://widenerenglish.wordpress.com/2012/10/01/mother-daughter-relationships-in-shakespeare/amp/. Accessed 28 June. 2022.

Bernstein, P. P. "Mothers and Daughters from Today's Psychoanalytic Perspective." *Psychoanalytic Inquiry.* 2004. http://dx.doi.org/10.1080/07351692409349106. Accessed 2 Jan. 2022.

Binns, Sarah. "Reversal and Threptra in Oedipus at Colonus". 2011. https://www.mcgill.ca. Accessed 2 Jan. 2022.

Briggs, Elizabeth Anne. *The Parent-Child Relationship and the Homeric Hero in the Iliad and Odyssey.* 2010. https://researchspace.ukzn.ac.za. Accessed 2 Jan. 2022.

Campbell, Joseph. "Myth and Dream." *The Hero with a Thousand Faces.* 3rd ed., New World Library, 2008.

Cantarella, Eva. "Fathers and Sons in Rome". *The Classical World*, Spring, 2003, Vol. 96, No. 3 (Spring, 2003), The Johns Hopkins University Press, 2003.

Crotty, K. *The Poetics of Supplication: Homer's Iliad and Odyssey*. Cornell University Press, 1994.

Deleuze, Gilles and Félix Guattari. *Anti-Oedipus: Capitalism and Schizophrenia.* University of Minnesota Press, 1972.

Donlan, W. "The Social Groups of Dark Age Greece." *Classical Philology.* Vol. 80, No. 4 (Oct., 1985). https://www.jstor.org › stable. Accessed 1 Jul. 2022.

Douglas, J. D., et al. "Ten Commandments," *New Bible Dictionary*, Second Edition, Tyndale House, 1982.

Eliade, Mircea. qtd. in Anon. "Chapter VIII: Lust or Strength Demeter/Persephone," https://zero-point.tripod.com/pantheon/Demeter.html. Accessed 24 May. 2022.

Eliot, qtd. in Heffernan, James A. W. *James Joyce's Ulysses: Remixing the Homeric Myth.* https://www.wondriumdaily.com/james-joyces-ulysses/. Accessed 10 Jul. 2022.

Ephesians. qtd. in Anon. "Family Relationships and Filial Duty." https://crossref-it.info/textguide/the-taming-of-the-shrew/43/3387. Accessed 29 June. 2022.

Euripides. *Medea and Other Plays*. Translated by Philip Vellacott, Penguin Classics, 1963.

Falkner, Thomas M. *The Poetics of Old Age in Greek Epic, Lyric and Tragedy.* University of Oklahoma Press, 1995.

Felson, N. "Paradigms of Paternity: Fathers, Sons and Athletic/Sexual Prowess in Homer's *Odyssey*". *Kazazis and Rengakos*. 1999. https://onlinelibrary.wiley.com>doi. Accessed 2 Jul. 2022.

———. "Threptra and Invincible Hands: The Father-Son Relationship in *Iliad.*" *Arethusa.* Vol. 24. John Hopkins University Press, 2002. https://muse.jhu.edu>. Accessed 2 June. 2022.

Finlay, R. A. "Patroklos, Achilles and Peleus: Fathers and Sons in the *Iliad*" 1980. https://msgrfarrellhs.org> Accessed 28 Jul. 2022.

Fernandes, Marie. "Myth and Cult in Literature." https://standrewscollege.ac.in/wp-content/uploads/2018/06/Myth-and-Cult-in-Literature.pdf. Accessed 1 Jul. 2022.

Finley, M. I. *The World of Odysseus*. Viking Press, 1954.

Flax, Jane. "Political Philosophy and the Patriarchal Unconscious: A Psychoanalytic Perspective on Epistemology and Metaphysics", in *Discovering Reality*. Edited by John Symons, University of Texas, 2003.

Freud, Sigmund. "On Dreams" in *Art in theory, 1900-1990: An Anthology of Changing Ideas.* Edited by Charles Harrison and Paul Wood, Blackwell Publishers Ltd, 1992.

———. qtd. in "Id, Ego, and Superego". https://www.simplypsychology.org/psyche.html. Accessed 19 May. 2022.

———. "Some Character Types met within Psycho – Analytic Work." *On the History of Psycho-Analytic Movement.* The Hogarth Press, 1916.

———. *The Complete Letters of Sigmund Freud to Wilhelm Fliess 1887-1904.* Translated and Edited by Jeffrey Maoussaieff Masson, The Belknap Press of Harvard University Press, 1985.

———. *The Interpretation of Dreams.* General Press, 2019.

Godley, A.D. trans. *Herodotus.* Harvard University Press, 1920.

Graves, Robert. *The Greek Myths.* Penguin Classics, 2011.

Green, Andre. *The Tragic Effect: The Oedipus Complex in Tragedy.* Cambridge, 1979.

Greene, T. *The Descent from Heaven: A Study in Epic Continuity.* Yale University Press, 1970.

Griffin, J. *Homer on Life and Death.* Clarendon Press, 1980.

Groddeck, Georg. "Peer Gynt." *Ibsen: A Collection of Critical Essays*, edited by Rolf Fjelde, Prentice Hall, 1995.

Halberstadt-Freud, Hendrika C. *Electra vs. Oedipus: The Drama of the Mother-Daughter Relationship.* Routledge, 2011.

*HESIOD. Theogony And Works and Day*s. Translated by M.L. West, Oxford University Press, 1988.

Hesiod and Homer. *Hesiod, The Homeric Hymns and Homerica.* Translated by Hugh G. Evelyn-White, William Heinemann Ltd., 1914.

Homer, "Hymn To Demeter." *Hymn To Demeter*. Translated by Hugh G. Evelyn White. Loeb Classical Library, http://www.sacre-texts.com/cla/demeter.htm>. Accessed 2 December. 2021.

———. *The Iliad.* Translated by E.V. Rieu. Penguin Classics, 2003.

———. *The Iliad of Homer.* Translated by Alexander Pope, The Project Gutenberg Ebook, 2006. http://www.gutenberg.org/license. Accessed 27 May. 2022.

———. *The Homeric Hymns*. Translated by Jules Cashford. Penguin Classics, 2003.

———. *The Odyssey*. Translated by E.V. Rieu. Penguin Classics, 2003.

———. *The Odyssey*. Translated by Robert Fagles. Penguin Classics, 1997.

Humphrey, Nicholas K. *Consciousness Regained.* Oxford UP, 1983.

Irigaray, Luce. *Speculum of the Other Woman*. Translated by Gillian C. Gill. Cornell University Press, 1974.

———. *This Sex Which is Not One*. Translated by Catherine Porter, Cornell University Press, 1977.

Jacobi, Jolande. *The Way of Individuation*. Harcourt Brace, 1967.

Joyce, James. *A Portrait of the Artist as a Young Man*, edited by. R.B. Kershner, Bedford St. Martins, 2006.

Jung, Carl Gustav. *Essays on a Science of Mythology*. Translated by R. F. C. Hull. Princeton University Press, 1967.

———. *Freud and Psychoanalysis. Collected Works, Vol. 4.* Pantheon, 1961.

———. *Man and His Symbols.* Bantam Doubleday Dell Publishing Group Inc, 1964.

———. *Symbols of Transformation: An Analysis of the Prelude to a Case of Schizophrenia*. Translated by R. F. C. Hull. Princeton University Press, 1976. https://the-eye.eu>public>concen.org. Accessed 29 Dec. 2021.

———. "The Psychological Aspects of the Kore". *Collected Works of C.G. Jung Vol.9 Part 1*. Edited by Gerhard Adler and R. F.C. Hull, https://doi.org/10.1515/9781400850969.182. Accessed 24 May. 2022.

———. *The Theory of Psychoanalysis*. Nervous and Mental Disease Publishing Co., 1901.

Kaivalya, Alanna. "Demeter and Persephone: A Prime Example of Borderline Personality Disorder in a Mother and Daughter Relationship." https://alannak.com. Accessed 2 June. 2022.

Keller, Mary Lynn. "The Eleusinian Mysteries of Demeter and Persephone: Fertility, Sexual and Rebirth." *Journal of Feminist Studies in Religion*. Indiana University Press, 1988. https://www.jstor.org/stable/25002068. Accessed 2 June. 2022.

Kirk, G. S. *The Iliad: A Commentary, II*. Cambridge Univ., 1990.

Klein, Melanie. *The Collected Writings of Melanie Klein*. Hogarth Press, 1921.

———. *The Psychoanalysis of Children*. W W Norton & Co., 1932.

———. "Notes on Some Schizoid Mechanisms". *Projective identification: The fate of a conc*ept. Edited by Elizabeth Spillius and Edna O'Shaughnessy, Routledge, 2012.

Knox, Bernard M. W. *The Heroic Temper: Studies in Sophoclean Tragedy*. University of California Press, 1964.

Lacan, Jacques. Écrits*: The First Complete Edition in English*. Translated by Bruce Fink, Héloïse Fink, Russell Grigg, W.W. Norton & Company, 2006.

———. *The Seminar. Book XI. The Four Fundamental Concepts of Psychoanalysis*. Translated by Alan Sheridan, Hogarth Press and Institute of Psycho-Analysis, 1977.

Lawrence, D. H. *Sons and Lovers*. A.I.T.B.S. Publishers, 2009.

Lawson, Christine Ann. Understanding the Borderline Mother: Helping Her Children Transcend the Intense, Unpredictable, and Volatile Relationship. Rowman & Littlefield, 2002.

Leach, Edmund. *Claude Levi-Strauss*. Viking, 1970.

Luke, Helen. "The Mother-Daughter Mysteries." *Dromenon*, 1982.

Malinowski, Bronislaw. *Sex and Repression in Savage Society*. Kegan Paul, Trench, & Trubner, 1927.

Makowski, John F. "Persephone, Psyche, and the Mother-Maiden Archetype." *Classical Outlook 26, American Classical Myth.* Lyola University. 1985. https://ecommons.luc.edu. Accessed 12 June. 2022.

Masek, Rosemary. *Women of England: From Anglo-Saxon Times to the Present.* Archon Books, 1979.

McBride, Kari B. *Domestic Arrangements in Early Modern England.* Duquesnes UP, 2002.

Morford, Mark P.O., and Robert J. Lenardon. *Classical Mythology.* Oxford University Press, 1999.

"Mourning Becomes Electra – Summary." Edited by Steven G. Kellman, eNotes.com, Inc., 2006. https://www.enotes.com/topics/mourning-becomes#summary-summary-summary-the-work. Accessed 10 Jul. 2022.

Mullahy, Patrick. "Oedipus: Myth and Complex- A Review of Psychoanalytic Theory." *The American Journal of Psychology.* University of Illinois Press, 1949. Accessed 28 June. 2022.

Neumann, Erich. *Amor and Psyche: The Psychic Development of the Feminine. A Commentary on the tale by Apuleius*. Translated by Ralph Manheim. Princeton University Press, 1971.

———. *The Great Mother*. Translated by Ralph Manheim. Princeton University Press, 1955.

Pindar. *Pindarπs Victory Song.* Translated by Frank J. Nisetich, Johns Hopkins 1980. https://web.as.miami.edu/personal/corax/pindar.html. Accessed 19 May. 2022.

Nussbaum, Martha C. and Juha Sihvola. Eds. *The Sleep of Reason: Erotic Experience and Sexual Ethics in Ancient Greece and Rome.* University of Chicago Press, 2013.

Patterson, C. B. *The Family in Greek History.* Harvard University Press, 1998.

Pratt, L. "The Parental Ethos of the *Iliad.*" *Hesperia Supplements.* The American School of Classical Studies at Athens, 2007. https://www.jstor.org/stable/20066781. Accessed 2 June. 2022.

Raaflaub, K. A. "Homeric Society." *A New Companion to Homer*. Edited by I. Morris & B. Powell, Brill, 1997.

Rayor, Diane J. *Homeric Hymn to Demeter*. Grand Valley State University, 1998.

Redfield, James M. *Nature and Culture in the Iliad: The Tragedy of Hector.* Chicago University Press, 1975.

Roth, Kimberlee, and Freda B. Friedman. *Surviving a Borderline Parent: How to Heal Your Childhood Wounds & Build Trust, Boundaries, and Self-esteem.* New Harbinger Publications, 2003.

Shakespeare, William. *The Tragedy of Hamlet, Prince of Denmark.* Simon & Schuster, 1992. *Folger Shakespeare Libra*ry, https://shakespeare.folger.edu/. Accessed 16 May. 2022.

———. *The Arden Shakespeare: Complete Works.* Edited by Richard Proudfoot, et al. Methuen Drama, 2001.

Seymour, T. D. *Life in the Homeric Age.* The Macmillan Company, 2004.

Singh, Sarup. *Family Relationships in Shakespeare and The Restoration Comedy of Manners*. Oxford UP, 1983.

Sophocles. *The Theban Plays*. Translated by Robert Fagles. The Penguin Group, 1982

———. *Electra and Other Plays*. Translated by David Raeburn. Penguin Classics, 2008.

———. *Sophocles I: Oedipus the King, Oedipus at Colonus, Antigone.* Translated and Edited by David Grene, Richmond Alexander Lattimore and Elizabeth Wyckoff, University of Chicago Press, 1954.

Strauss, B. S. *Fathers and Sons in Athens: Ideology and Society in the Era of the Peloponnesian War.* Princeton University Press, 1993.

Thompson, William Irwin. *The Time Falling Bodies Take to Light.* St. Martin's, 1981.

Tsoutsouki, C. "The Father-Son Relationship in the Iliad: The Case of Priam-Hector Introduction", 2014. www.rosetta.bham.ac.uk>tsoutsouki. Accessed 29 June. 2022.

Twentieth Century Interpretations of The Tempest. Edited by Hallett Smith, Prentice-Hall, 1969.

Vernant, Jean-Pierre. *The Forest of Symbols: Aspects of Ndembu Ritual.* Cornell University Press, 1967.

Walde, Christine. "Dream Interpretation in a Prosperous Age? Artemidorus, the Greek Interpreter of Dreams." *Dream Cultures: Explorations in the Comparative History of Dreaming.* Edited by D. Shulman and G. Strousma, Oxford University Press, 1999.

Walsh, P.G. *The Roman Novel*. Cambridge Univ. Press, 1970.

Willner, Dorothy. "The Oedipus Complex, Antigone, and Electra: The Woman as Hero and Victim." *American Anthrologist*, 1982. https://www.jstor.org/stable/675950. Accessed 2 June. 2022.

Zajchowski, Stephanie. "Demeter and Persephone as Temenos: A Perspective of Understanding Postpartum Depression." *Mythological Studies Journal*. Vol. 5. https://journals.sfu.ca.pgi. Accessed 20 Sep. 2022.

Zeitlin, Froma. "Cultic Models of the Female: Rites of Dionysus and Demeter" *Arethusa,15.* The Johns Hopkins University Press, 1982. https://www.jstor.org/stable/26308107. Accessed 16 Jul. 2022.